THE BROTHAHOOD OF KINGS

Empowering Black Men To Embrace Authentic Masculinity

Coach Michael Taylor

W/ Jermaine Johnson - Paul Randolph Newell - Greg Reimoku Smith

The Brothahood of Kings

Published by Creation Publishing Group LLC

www.creationpublishing.com

© 2023 Michael Taylor
ISBN # 978-1-7366369-7-8

Library of Congress Control Number: 2023900582

All rights reserved. No part of this book may be used, reproduced, stored in, introduced into a retrieval system, or transmitted in any form or by any means without the express written consent of the publisher.

Published and printed in the United States of America.

Table of Contents

Foreword v

Acknowledgments vii

Introduction 1

Chapter 1: There Is No Black Male Crisis 9

Chapter 2: Redefining Manhood and Masculinity 27

Chapter 3: Zen and The Art of Mature Masculinity 55

Chapter 4: A Brotha's Trauma 69

Chapter 5: You Must Make Peace With Your Past 81

Chapter 6: You Must Create A Positive Support Network .. 105

Chapter 7: Prioritize Relationships 121

Chapter 8: How Do You See God? 147

Chapter 9: Spiritual Laws and Principles 169

Chapter 10: The Four Pillars Of An Extraordinary Life 191

Chapter 11: Don't Forget To Have Some Fun 211

Chapter 12: Be Willing To Serve 221

    Bio's 229

    Resources 237

Foreword

I have been writing and speaking about black male empowerment for the past twenty-eight years. Despite mainstream media, it is my contention that black men are thriving and experiencing unprecedented levels of success today. I do not accept the media-generated narratives that suggest black men are an endangered species. I am personally filled with optimism because I believe the key to our success lies in our willingness to change our mindsets about what is possible for black men, and we all have the ability to change our mindsets.

The difficult part is getting black men to change their mindsets, which unfortunately can be extremely difficult to do because far too many black men have fallen victim to a negative mindset and attitude due to accepting negative media stereotypes.

I'm reminded of a quote from R. Buckmeister Fuller, which says, "You never change things by fighting the existing reality. To change something, build a new model that makes the existing model obsolete."

Foreword

Therefore, I took his advice and decided to create a new model for black men, and I launched a movement called Shatter The Stereotypes. I created the movement as a resource for black men to support and empower them to change their mindsets and to provide them with the tools to succeed in all areas of their lives. This movement consists of a book I wrote titled: Shattering Black Male Stereotypes, and it also includes a podcast and television show titled, Shatter The Stereotypes.

To continue building this new model for black men, I've partnered with three very good friends of mine, Paul Newell, Reimoku (Greg Smith), and Jermaine Johnson. We have put together a new movement called The Brothahood of Kings, and this book is an expression of our collaboration. The Brothahood of Kings intends to empower black men to engage in their personal growth and development. We will accomplish our intention through a series of books, online courses, Webinars, and live seminars.

Therefore, if you are a man of color looking for a resource that supports you in becoming the best version of yourself, you've come to the right place. This book and this movement were designed specifically for you, and we would like to extend an invitation for you to join The Brothahood of Kings. (www.brothahoodofkings.com)

Acknowledgments

As an author of twelve books, I always begin by acknowledging the Divine Intelligence that created and is still creating this amazing Universe we live in. I have come to know this Divine Intelligence as the source of my creativity and passion for making a difference in the world. It is my connection to this Intelligence that drives everything I do. I've heard some people say they are just the vessels through which God expresses itself, and I wholeheartedly agree with that statement. As a matter of fact, I would suggest Divine Intelligence is actually expressing itself through me as me. I am simply a divine expression of this Divine Intelligence. I also believe you are too! Every human being is a divine expression of God, and it is our responsibility to connect with and express our God-given gifts and talents to work hand in hand with God to make the world a better place.

As I reflect on the past thirty years of my life, I can see the Divine Hand that has guided me along my journey. It is nothing short of a miracle that I have become an entrepreneur, author of twelve books, motivational speaker, podcaster, TV host, and certified life coach with no formal training or college degrees.

Acknowledgments

The only thing I had was a vision of building an extraordinary life, and I now see how Divine Intelligence guided me to manifest my vision.

Therefore, I choose to acknowledge Divine Intelligence and say thank you for this wonderful gift called life. The best way to express my gratitude is by sharing my gifts and talents with the world to make it a better place while acknowledging the Source, which I choose to call Divine Intelligence.

In June 2002, I participated in a weekend workshop called The New Warrior Training Adventure. (www.mkp.org) The workshop is designed to support men in embracing a new paradigm of masculinity in which men learn to let go of antiquated roles of manhood and masculinity. It was a transformational experience that positively changed my view of manhood. There were approximately 80-100 men on the weekend, and I was the only black man in attendance. Although this didn't bother me, I wondered why there weren't other black men participating.

After the graduation ceremony, I met three black men who had completed the training earlier. We quickly became friends and decided to create a group for black male graduates of the program. We began by meeting once a week and creating a safe space in which we could speak openly and honestly about anything going on in our lives, including the good, the bad, and the ugly. It was my first experience in a men's group, and it allowed me to heal, grow, and integrate some things I learned from the workshop. After a couple of years, we started meeting less frequently, but our meetings continued to be a safe space for our growth and transformation. After more than twenty years, we still meet at least once a year to connect and support each other. So, at this time, I would like to acknowledge Judge Mattocks, Russell Richard, and Ernest Patterson. These men are my true brothers; I love them and would trust them with my life.

During one of our meetings, we made a commitment to make sure more black men could experience the camaraderie and growth we shared in our group. We each dedicated our lives to sharing our experience and wisdom with other black men, and each of us has kept that commitment. Judge and Ernest are facilitators of The New Warrior Training Adventure, and Russell is a psychotherapist who helps men deal with their mental and emotional health. I share my wisdom with black men through writing books and hosting a podcast and TV show specifically for black men called Shatter The Stereotypes.

So to my brothers, Judge, Russell, and Ernest, I just want to say I love you and am grateful to have you in my life. We said we would change the world, and we have!

Acknowledgments

While scrolling through Facebook, I watched a video with a guy named Paul Newell. He was talking about the challenges of being a man, and I deeply resonated with his message. We connected on Facebook, and I enjoyed watching and commenting on his videos. It turned out he was also a graduate of The New Warrior Training Adventure, so our relationship deepened. It turned out that we were both members of an online group for black men, and we began collaborating on a couple of projects.

Another member of that group was Jermaine Johnson. I had worked with Jermaine previously on a project, and he also was a New Warrior graduate. Jermaine has the energy of a man you instantly trust and he exudes integrity and is the type of guy you just love to hang around.

I met Reimoku (Greg Smith) online and was intrigued by his spiritual insights. He was a practicing Buddhist who I invited to be featured on my podcast. I felt an immediate connection with him, and we became good friends. Coincidentally, he was also friends with Paul Newell.

In March of 2022, the four of us came together to collaborate on a new movement on which Paul and Reimoku had been working. We decided to name the movement, The Brothahood of Kings, and the intention was to provide men of color with resources to support them in embodying authentic masculinity. This book is one of those resources. So I would like

The Brothahood of Kings

to acknowledge Paul, Reimoku, and Jermaine for their contributions to this book and for their commitment to empowering black men. We are committed to changing the world one man at a time, and it is my absolute honor to collaborate with them on this new movement. (www.brothahoodofkings.com)

Last but definitely not least, I'd like to acknowledge you, the reader, for reading this book. Reading a book like this takes incredible courage, so let me begin by acknowledging your bravery. Truth be told, for us to succeed as black men, one of the first things we must be willing to do is face our fears and move past them. By reading this book, that is exactly what you're doing.

So let me begin by welcoming you to the Brothahood of Kings! I'm glad you've decided to join us, and I'm looking forward to seeing you grow into the man you were born to be. Rest assured, this book can definitely help you do that.

Introduction

by
Judge Mattocks

Much of my life was spent in search of something. Many experiences weave a tapestry of love. A love that I only dreamed of for decades. Love that was always available and rarely accessed. Being driven by fear, shame, and cowardness. I fell prey to depression, arrogance and self-importance. I hid, denied, and repressed my truth every day to avoid what I considered to be the harsh judgments of others.

I grew up believing that I could never measure up to my cousins, especially my male cousins. The harder I tried the more miserably I failed. The only place I excelled during my early years was in school. Where in my judgments, I was being held back so the others my age could catch up. That's what my younger self believed for way too long.

The last thing I said to my brother before he ran into oncoming traffic and became a statistic was: "Don't come over here

Introduction

just because it's raining. Go back with your buddy Bruce like you've been doing". And five minutes later he was prone in a puddle of water after being struck by a drunken driver. I carried that guilt for nearly fifty years. My life is a litany of opportunities to learn yet another lesson. There are four children, two divorces, countless affairs and debts that can't be repaid except to pay them forward. A concept I have embraced. The tapestry of my life before September of 2000 prepared me for an experience that lives deeply within me to this moment.

I was struggling in a 12-step program. The sixth step wasn't resonating within me. My sponsor, Steven K, shared with me his experience of a Men's Weekend that he believed could help me with a breakthrough. Being ready for some movement in my recovery I agreed to go and attended the first available seminar. Little did I know that "my life would be forever changed".

That weekend started a weekend of awareness, commitment, and progress in loving myself. With everything I gained on that weekend something truly important was missing. In order to participate regularly I had to abandon my community yet again. Abandonment has been one of the themes of my growth. I found that I was doing everything I judged my father, grandfather, male relatives for doing.

The dilemma of leaving a container where I was gaining respect for one that called me back to my old dangerously addictive patterns. The loneliness of being an only (black, female, Asian, gay, etc.) person of any persuasion. I had become attracted to Man Kind Project (MKP) and readily found a lack of other men of obvious African ancestry readily accessible to me. There were rumors that Chicago had a haven of us and that was a world away from me.

On the path to responsibility, I met a few pioneers and asked about those that were in my area. I learned of the decision of the pioneers from Houston lost their leader and were attracted to the faction of men that created their own organization based in Memphis.

My thirst for answers led me and three other men of obvious African ancestry, (Ernest Patterson, Michael Taylor and Russell Richard) to venture a road trip to experience Inward Journey's training the, Under Ground Railroad Odyssey (UGRRO). We are now affectionately known as the "four amigos". We formed a weekly group, "Friday Night Lights" that met for 3 – 4 years.

As our lives changed, Friday became a difficult day for each of us and we vowed to remain. We now meet yearly for a meal; and we still support each other's projects as requested.

My quest included co-creating community among black men doing this work. Inward Journey clearly was doing that and doing it well. However, we weren't in Memphis and the pioneers of IJ from Houston weren't interested in working with men associated with MKP. Especially, if MKP was insisting on being gay accepting. I was really experiencing *being between a rock and a hard place.*

Introduction

Everywhere I went there were one or two MOAA men now more commonly known as BIPOC men to include most men marginalized by race, nationality, and spiritual beliefs. I was the first BIPOC man in Houston to get certified to lead the weekend training which meant I was invited to many communities to make a plan to look at the lack of diversity within MKP. I joined a status which included being among the other BIPOC certified men within MKP.

After many unaddressed micro-cuts men adopted a stance of not leading on a training where the community didn't have any BIPOC members without inviting another BIPOC man to join the leader. I adopted this policy and that became me building acquaintance all over the network that have some have become friends, brothas, and colleagues.

I began spreading the messages of not being on the staff of a weekend where you are the only BIPOC staffer. I started collecting contact information and started conversations about the questions of why to invite more BIPOC men to checkout MKP. I was so surprised when men were astonished to hear of others even in their communities. That led me to the fact that MKP purposely didn't keep demographic information about one's ethnicity. It was said to be intentional so MKP wouldn't appear to be exclusive in anyway.

The impact on BIPOC men is, we didn't know we each existed. If I went to a center and asked to have the men of African ancestry contact me, I would be told the center didn't keep that data on its members. I began to observe that as BIPOC members of MKP, we were not available to support each other and many of us would go years without fully taking advantage of the possibility of personal growth within our communities. I found a defunct email list where BIPOC men had used before I became a member. I worked with the provider of that list to establish a forum for men to connect.

The list had gone for years without use. The administrator of the list had burned bridges with the men and many didn't wish to connect with him again. I used the list to begin a campaign of connecting BIPOC men within MKP with each other to form a coalition to support each other. The original list was a forum call AFAM for African American. I needed a different designation to separate my vision from the message men carried about AFAM. I wanted the name to have an immediate reference to the principles I had adopted as a New Warrior and recognize my BIPOC status. I had started identifying as an American of some obvious African ancestry.

Something that does have a convenient acronym. I needed something that bespoke African American with pop. Something that declared us as male centered and community based.

I put the call out. I would host a Zoom call every second and fourth Thursday night until further notice and I set up an automatic notice to go twice monthly reminding men that I would be on Zoom. I needed to choose a time that could best

Introduction

serve men across 4 time zones. 8PM ET seem to fit the bill the best and so I began. Slowly men visited and we began inviting others we ran into and new men as they were initiated were given word of mouth of my desire to connect with them.

At first my name Judge intrigued men. Who is this guy and why connect with him. Honestly, I believe me outside of large metro areas were the first draw. We hungered to connect with others like us. We met rigorously for the first year 2016. We continued to grow, and I had an amazing conversation with a man named, D Moment, and he decided to join the cause and the rest became history. We still didn't have a name for ourselves. I spent a week or so over what to call my brotherhood of men. It came to me in an instant. Brotha...for an Ebonics description and Hood for the community reference. Putting them together was the real inspiration for **BrothaHood**.

What is a BrothaHood? It is a community of men of some African ancestry (MOSAA) working together to transform themselves, their narratives of themselves; into a network of experiences, talents, and determination to change the world. It is a code of honor. A commitment to our community to be productive and useful among the tribe. We exist invisibly while constantly enduring negativity and scorn. We dare not teach our young to ignore the police. Forever vigilant we do everything from removing the trash to the CEO. One of us has recently occupied the Oval Office and represented with dignity.

The Brothahood of Kings

Until recently we have been fragmented and the time for Ubuntu has come. Time to remember our bodies are the gift from mother Earth and the spirit that sustains that body lives within each of us. It is imperative that we care for and protect our Mother and honor the spirit we each share. The spirit that created this Earth, that holds our sun in place, that constructed the worlds according to the laws of physics beyond the full understanding of any of us live today. It is: "The Spirit of Ubuntu."

The call to those who have the ears to hear has been and is being made. There is no way we will abandon our women. There are pathways where we meet; endeavors we must collaborate equally, especially in recognizing our leaders. There must be pathways that are masculine oriented and other that are feminine in nature, moving toward the time our intersexed offspring are respected.

This call is to all. Don't forget Marvin's question: "What's Going On?" In the pages of this book I hope you find some of what attracted me along this journey. Let the pages offer you a connection with likeminded men. Maybe one of you will resonate with one of the many personal stories' men will share. I hope that at least you will find it stirring. That some emotional reaction gets triggered. Those that take this opportunity to do a self-examination of their personal integrity and may want support or to support others to live integral lives.

Enjoy this morsel of fresh air. Welcome to the Brothahood!

"Change will not come if we wait for some other person or if we wait for some other time. We are the ones we've been waiting for. We are the change that we seek."
- President Barack Obama

Chapter 1

There Is No Black Male Crisis

On May 25th, 2020, George Floyd attempted to purchase some cigarettes with a counterfeit twenty-dollar bill from a convenience store in Minneapolis. The police were called, and within seventeen minutes, George Floyd had been pinned down on the ground by Officer Derek Chauvin. A video shows Officer Chauvin with his knee on George's neck for eight minutes and 46 seconds. During that time, George continuously told the officer he couldn't breathe, and even after he went unconscious, the officer kept his knee on his neck for a full minute and 20 seconds. Sadly, George Floyd died, and the world had front-row seats to a white police officer killing a black man on national television.

The first time I saw the video of George Floyd, I had to turn it off. It hurt too much for me to watch it. I was deeply saddened for a couple of reasons. Number one, I was deeply saddened by the brutality of his murder. How could a police officer be so cold and inhumane to another human being? Number two, I was deeply saddened knowing that young black men would see it, and it would perpetuate the stereotype that black men are an endangered species.

In my book *Shattering Black Male Stereotypes*, I identified what I consider to be the ten most destructive media-generated illusions about black men. The number one illusion is black men are an endangered species. Police brutality is the primary reason this illusion is perpetuated, followed by gun violence.

I'm reminded of a conversation I overheard between two apparently well-educated, well-spoken professional black men. They were having a conversation about the eradication of black men from society. I walked over to their table to ask them if they truly believed what they were saying, and one of the guys looked at me and said, "Don't you watch the news? I believe in twenty years, all black men will be dead or in jail."

These men had accepted the illusion that black men were an endangered species, and based on their conversation, they did not believe it was possible for black men to truly succeed in America. Seeing how George Floyd was killed, it's no wonder some black men feel endangered.

Contrary to what you may see in the media or what you may believe, it is my contention that black men are thriving and experiencing unprecedented levels of success today. I like to think of myself as an irrepressible optimist with a passion for the impossible, and yet my optimism is sometimes vilified by some black men. Because of my optimism, I have been accused of being a sellout and out of touch with the reality of being a Black man in America. I have been accused of denying the impact that slavery and racism have had on black men simply because I believe every black man has the capacity to create the life of his dreams. I do not deny the challenges; I simply choose to focus my attention on things I have control over. For example, I cannot control what the media will show about black men. However, I have complete control over how I react to what the media shows. Therefore, I simply focus my attention on finding solutions to the challenges we face instead of placing blame on the media and racism. This doesn't deny racism exists; it simply allows me to take hundred percent responsibility for my life and everything that shows up in it.

That said, I'd like to share why I believe there is no black male crisis and how I came to this conclusion.

First of all, I'm a child of the sixties, and I vividly remember the heights of the civil rights movement. I remember having race riots in elementary school where the black kids were on one side of the cafeteria and the white kids were on the other side. I remember an incidence when a black kid walked over to the white side and was attacked, and all hell broke loose.

I'll never forget jumping up from the table, running over to help the black kid, and getting into a fight with a white kid. This was in elementary school!

After school, I remember asking my grandfather why white people and black people didn't get along and he told me he didn't have an answer but believed God had a plan and somehow would fix everything.

Another thing I remember from the 60s was watching television on our tiny black and white thirteen-inch TV. I remember what a big deal it was whenever a black person was on television and how my grandmother would react. She would get on the phone and call several different people to make sure they were watching, and the next time those friends came over, they would sit around the table and talk about how great it was to see black people on television.

My most painful experience of blatant racism occurred when I was seventeen. I was in high school, and I met and fell in love with my high school sweetheart. She was a wonderful supportive, caring person that incidentally happened to be white. When we met, she was somewhat of a wild child. She came from a pretty wealthy family yet hated her father and was into drugs and rebellion. She was a C and D student that liked to skip school and hang out at the beach with her friends. After going out with her for a while, I convinced her to turn her life around and give up skipping school and abusing drugs.

The Brothahood of Kings

She changed her attitude and became an A and B student. We were extremely close and shared that high school infatuated kind of love that feels so deep that it stays with you for a lifetime. After going out with her for over a year, her father found out that we were dating. One night I got a phone call from him, and it was obvious that he was unhappy.

As he began speaking, I knew I needed to keep my cool and not disrespect him. I listened to his objections and allowed him to get everything off his chest. When he finished, I made the mistake of telling him that he did not have the right to decide whom his daughter should date. I tried to convince him that I had been a good influence on his daughter and that he should be happy that she was doing so well. I hoped I could get him to understand that I was a good guy who was actually good for his daughter. Of course, he could not hear a word I was saying. He was adamant about the fact that he knew what was best for his daughter, and I was just some young punk trying to take advantage of his little girl. After screaming his disapproval of our relationship for several minutes, he said something that caught me off guard. Although I knew he was angry, I did not expect to hear these words, "There is no way that I will allow my daughter to date a nigger. I will kill you before I let that happen." Although the words were painful, it was the venomous feeling of anger and hatred that came through the phone that ripped out my heart. Even today, almost forty-six years later, I can still feel the hatred in his words. His anger came from deep within his soul, and it was apparent that it wasn't just about me but all black people.

There Is No Black Male Crisis

As I sat there in disbelief, I immediately went numb. A part of me wanted to defend myself, curse at him, and retaliate in some way. I quickly subdued my initial feeling of anger to avoid getting into a shouting match. Another part of me was terrified because I did not know whether or not he would actually attempt to take my life. But the feeling I remember most after his comment was sadness. I remember a sinking feeling in my gut resulting from being invalidated as a human being. I knew that he viewed me as less than a man, and in his mind, I was not good enough for his daughter simply because I was black. It was dehumanizing and demoralizing. How could this man hate me so much and not know anything about me? How could he pass judgment without ever seeing or speaking to me? Why could he not see my positive influence on his daughter? Why was I not allowed the opportunity to meet with him and talk to him so that he could see how much I really cared about his daughter and that I intended to simply love and support her?

Despite this experience and several other experiences dealing with racism, I have never felt angry or bitter toward white people. As I reflect on my sixty-three years on this earth and the challenges I've personally overcome, I remain optimistic that we are headed in the right direction regarding race relations. It's pretty obvious that we still have a long way to go, but based on the trajectory we've been on for the last two-hundred-and-fifty years, I believe we are moving in the right direction.

But what about the black male crisis?

The Brothahood of Kings

To fully understand why there really isn't a black male crisis anymore, it's important to look back through history. Obviously, there was a time in this country's history when things like slavery and lynching were a real threat to black men. Currently, police brutality, high incarceration rates, and gun violence are definitely impacting black men's mortality. Although these challenges are very real, the data does not support the idea that black men are endangered and in crisis. Yes, there are challenges, but collectively speaking, black men are thriving.

To find where the black male crisis story began, you have to go back to the '60s and '70s. Back then, black organizations were attempting to get funding to help eradicate things like poverty and violence. In order to receive funding, they had to convince nonprofits that there was a need for their services, so they had to prove to the nonprofit that there was a problem and that they were the solution to that problem. Therefore, they compiled as much negative data about black males as they could in order to receive funding. In their attempt to receive funding, they began sharing their negative statistics with mainstream media. Since mainstream media thrives on sensationalism and negativity, the media used every opportunity to spread the news that there was a black male crisis. Because of social media and twenty-four-hour news cycles, in addition to this country's addiction to negative news, we are constantly bombarded with this misinformation, and too many people have concluded there is a black male crisis.

There Is No Black Male Crisis

I'm certain there are "experts" who would disagree with me and provide their own statistics to support their beliefs that there really is a black male crisis, but I stand by my assertion - there is really no such thing as a black male crisis now in 2023.

Although I'm not a fan of statistics because they can be misconstrued to say whatever the author is trying to say based on their point of view, I'd like to share some data from a report called: Black Men Making It In America – The Engines of Economic Success for Black Men in America by W. Bradford Wilcox, Wendy R. Wang, and Ronald B. Mincy.

Here are some of their findings from the report:

- **Black men's economic standing.** More than one-in-two black men (57%) have made it into the middle class or higher as adults today, up from 38% in 1960, according to a new analysis of Census data. And the share of black men who are poor has fallen from 41% in 1960 to 18% in 2016. So, a substantial share of black men in America are realizing the American Dream—at least financially—and a clear majority are not poor.

- **The institutional engines of black men's success.** As expected, higher education and full-time work look like engines of success for black men in America. But three other institutions that tend to get less attention in our current discussions of race—the U.S. military, the black church, and marriage—also appear to play significant roles in black men's success. For instance, black men who served in the military are more likely than those who did not to be in the middle class when they reach mid-life (54% vs. 45%), according to our new analysis of the National Longitudinal Survey of Youth (NLSY79). Black men who frequently attended church services at a young age are also more likely to reach the middle class or higher when they are in their fifties: 53% of those men who attended church as young men made it, compared to 43% who did not. Finally, about 70% of married black men are in the middle class, compared to only 20% of never-married black men and 44% of divorced black men.

- **The importance of individual agency.** Black men who score above average in their sense of agency—measured by reports that they feel like they are determining the course of their own lives versus feeling like they do not have control over the direction of their lives—as young men or teenagers in the late 1970s are more likely to be prosperous later in life. Specifically, 52% of black men who had a higher sense of agency as young men made it into at least the middle class when they reached age 50, compared to 44% of their peers who did not have that sense of agency.

Instead of relying on statistics and expert reports, here are some reasons I'm extremely optimistic about the future for black men and race relations as a whole.

I currently host a podcast called Shatter The Stereotypes. The podcast intends to showcase and highlight black men who are doing remarkable things in the world. I have done well over a hundred interviews with black men from around the globe. I've interviewed spine surgeons, entrepreneurs, authors, therapists, actors, mayors, thought leaders and influencers, life coaches, engineers, motivational speakers, mentors, and White House Medical Officers, to name a few. Each time I interview these men, I am optimistic because of their intelligence, passion, purpose, and commitment to doing their part in making the world a better place. These men confirm that black men are thriving in all segments of society, even though you may not see their stories in mainstream media.

This is why it is so important for us to have our own media outlets. It is our responsibility to share our stories and to dispel the stereotypes perpetuated by mainstream media.

Another reason for my optimism is my own observations about what I see black men accomplishing today. For example, although I'm not heavily involved with politics, I was inspired to see Hakeem Jeffries become the first black male Speaker of the House in the US and Wes Moore become the first black male Governor of Maryland. These men were elected in 2022 and will take office in 2023.

If I'm going to talk about politics, I would be remiss if I didn't mention President Barrack Obama. Before he ran for president, I had no idea who he was. But his presidency confirms that anything is possible for black men if they put their minds to it. He was the epitome of intelligence, leadership, integrity, compassion, and grace, and he is definitely one of my favorite role models.

Did you hear the story of the brother from Nigeria named Dr. Oluyinka O. Olutoye? He removed a baby from the womb for twenty minutes, removed a tumor (while she was 23 weeks old), and then placed the baby back into the womb, and the baby was born healthy. Following his role in the groundbreaking surgery, Olutoye was appointed Surgeon-In-Chief at Nationwide Children's Hospital in the U.S. He now leads one of the world's largest children's hospital surgery departments. Absolutely amazing accomplishment!

As someone who loves science, I must admit my man crush for Neil DeGrasse Tyson, who happens to be a world-famous astrophysicist. I love listening to him speak about science and space, and he inspires me to reach for the stars and know that anything is possible.

As an entrepreneur, I am truly inspired by billionaire Robert Smith who paid off 34 million dollars of student loans for some Morehouse College students. He is the founder of the investment firm Vista Equity Partners, and he has a bachelor's degree in chemical engineering from Cornell University and an MBA from Columbia University.

As a movie lover, I have to shout out to Ryan Coogler, an American film director, producer, and screenwriter of Black

Panther and Wakanda Forever, which was the sequel. To date, Black Panther is number 15 on the list of top grossing films of all time, with gross revenue of over 1,347,597,973 dollars.

One of my favorite spiritual teachers is Michael Bernard Beckwith. He is a New Thought minister, author, founder, and spiritual director of the Agape International Spiritual Center in Beverly Hills, California. His teachings have been instrumental in me finding my own truth about God and creating an intimacy and connection with God, which is the foundation of my spirituality. He reaches millions of people around the globe with his powerful ministry and message.

As I look over these black men's accomplishments, it confirms that black men are thriving and experiencing unprecedented levels of success in the world today. We can do more than singing, dancing, and playing sports, and these few examples confirm this.

If I had to pinpoint the most important reason I remain optimistic about the future for black men, it would have to be my belief in the Divine Intelligence that created this Universe. In her groundbreaking book, Conscious Evolution, Barbara Marx Hubbard theorizes that human beings are still evolving. In the book, she states they are evolving from Homo-Sapiens to what she calls Homo-Universalis. Humans aren't evolving physically; they are evolving in consciousness.

Here is an excerpt from my book *Shattering Black Male Stereotypes* that will shed light on how humans are evolving.

The Brothahood of Kings

"With that being said, I wanted to share my thoughts about what my friend said about America being a racist country. It is my fervent belief that, without question, America is not a racist country. Are there racists that inhabit the US? Of course! The problem, as I see it, is we tend to refer to America as though it were a person. When people talk about the atrocities of slavery and discrimination, they refer to America as though it were a single person that was acting out on its own and causing these things to happen. We must accept that America comprises a diverse group of people who make up this great country. So America is simply a reflection of the consciousness of the people who live here. Since the majority of people living in the US, for the most part, have been white people (except when they first invaded America), this country has what I call a Collective White Belief System (CWBS). The CWBS has controlled this country for a very long time, but as the country has become more diverse, the CWBS is losing its influence and power.

When people talk about institutionalized racism and white privilege, they speak of the CWBS. It is a belief system based on white superiority that goes back hundreds of years. Another reason for my optimism is the fact that each generation moves further and further away from the CWBS. During the '60s and the Civil Rights Movement, the CWBS began shifting. The pioneers of the civil rights movement convinced enough white people that segregation and the treatment of people of color were wrong. This was no easy task. Changing the CWBS wasn't easy. That's why there were lunch counter sit-ins. That's why there was a march on Washington. That's why Dr. King's dream speech was so important. In order to shift the CWBS, a tipping point had to be reached, and once it did, things began to change.

So, what is the tipping point? Some people believe that once 51 percent of the population agrees on a new belief, then that belief changes the collective consciousness of the country. Using the example of the Civil Rights Movement, once 51 percent of white people changed their minds, then the CWBS changed, and the civil rights movement was accepted, and it changed the country.

Despite the apparent racial conflict that is still going on in this country, I believe that the CWBS is still being broken down, and this country can achieve racial harmony. As a matter of fact, I believe it's inevitable. There is always chaos before creation, and the current racial chaos we're experiencing will eventually lead to unity. You may be asking why I believe this, and you may believe that I am a pie-in-the-sky-dreamer, but it is my belief that there is divine order in the Universe and that power that is greater than myself is orchestrating the entire cosmos. This Divine Intelligence has an intention: to create heaven right here on earth and nothing can thwart that intention.

This does not mean that the CWBS does not exist. Quite the contrary. It still exists and still influences the minds and hearts of many people in this country. Proof of this can be found in our former president. It can also be found in racially motivated attacks on people of color. It can be found when white police officers kill black men and are acquitted of any crime, despite irrefutable evidence. It can be found in the disproportionate coverage of negative stories about black men. It is alive and well in this country, but as mentioned, I see the light at the end of the tunnel, and I am absolutely certain that the CWBS can be changed to the Collective Universal Belief System in which all human beings are accepted for who they are, and their diversity is celebrated.

It's been said that the first step in solving a problem is admitting you have one. To get rid of the CWBS, we must be willing to admit that it exists. Since the media contributes so much to our beliefs and perpetuates so many stereotypes, it's important for us to acknowledge that most people who control our media are white. They are driven by the CWBS, and although they may not be intentionally trying to hurt black people or hold them back, the result is still the same. They are contributing to the negative stereotypes of black men. So rather than call them racists, I will assert that they are biased based on the CWBS. In order for them to change that bias, we must continue to bring it to their attention by speaking out against the unequal coverage of black men and violence and challenging them to showcase the positive stories as equally as they do the negative ones.

But even more importantly, we must ensure that we share our positive stories with the world. Just like the CWBS exists, so does the Collective Black Belief System. Unfortunately, the CBBS can be even more destructive than the CWBS.

This is true because in many cases, the CBBS is attacking the CWBS for its unfair portrayal of black people, and yet at the same time, our media is filled with as much negativity as the white media. The constant barrage and attack of the CWBS perpetuate the idea that "all" white people and institutions are working against black people, and it creates feelings of powerlessness and victimization. The CWBS promotes an "us versus them" belief system, which creates anger, frustration, and division.

The one thing the CWBS refuses to acknowledge is the fact that collectively speaking, America loves violence. This is evidenced by the movies we watch, the music we listen to, the books and magazines we read, and of course, the news we watch. Just take a moment and think about the successful movies, music, and magazines in America. The majority of them are overwhelmingly violent and negative. Companies create products and services based on demand; if the demand isn't there, they would stop creating the content. So who are the people who are demanding this type of content? Since black people only make up approximately 13% of America, you can rest assured that we aren't responsible for this obsession with violence. The violence is driven by the CWBS simply because they are the majority of people who are demanding this content.

Since the CWBS thrives on violence and negativity, the key to our success lies in our ability and willingness to disengage from the CWBS and make sure we are not contributing to the violence and negativity ourselves. We must be willing to move past the negative media-generated stereotypes and provide ourselves with the resources to help us overcome the multiplicity of challenges we face to start building a brighter future for humanity as a whole."

Human evolution is my primary reason for optimism about the future. Divine Intelligence is the driving force of this evolution, and I believe the intention is for human beings to one day evolve to a point where they recognize their oneness, and race will no longer be an issue. We will evolve to the point where all humans recognize there is only one race which is the human race, and as John Lennon so eloquently stated, *"You may say I'm a dreamer, but I'm not the only one. I hope one day you'll join us and the world will be as one."*

Will this happen in my lifetime? Probably not. But if I look at the trajectory we've been on for the past 250 thousand years, I remain optimistic that it is inevitable.

So, the next time you hear someone say there is a black male crisis, remember the words of Public Enemy, "Don't believe the hype!"

I believe the greatest challenge we have on the planet right now is to redefine manhood and masculinity."
- Coach Michael Taylor

Chapter 2

Redefining Manhood and Masculinity

Back in the seventies, Hollywood released a series of movies called "blaxploitation films." The movies glamorized black men as pimps, gangsters, and drug dealers and definitely perpetuated negative stereotypes about black men. I was around fifteen when movies like Superfly, The Mac, and Black Caesar came out, and I had no idea of the negative impact those films had on the black male psyche. All I knew at the time was that I wanted to be cool like some of the characters, and I chose the nickname Superfly while I was in junior high. I remember wearing platform shoes and bell-bottomed pants and having a big afro with my afro pick stuck in my hair. I even had a nametag with Superfly on it. All of my friends called me Superfly, so I didn't see it as anything negative at the time.

Redefining Manhood and Masculinity

My family lived in government housing, and my closest friends also chose nicknames based on those blaxploitation films. A common denominator for most of us was that we didn't have fathers at home, so we chose movie characters as our role models. In some ways, watching those films laid the foundation for what it meant to be a man for us.

If you look closely, it should be easy to recognize how the media impacts our views and beliefs about what it means to be a man. During the '70s, the movies promoted the idea that to be a man, you had to have money, cars, women, and sex. If you listen to rap music now, you should notice it promotes the same thing. Unfortunately, too many men embrace the media version of manhood and masculinity, which is why so many of us are unhappy.

I mentioned in the quote preceding this chapter that I believe the greatest challenge we have today is redefining manhood and masculinity. This has nothing to do with race. It has everything to do with men trapped in antiquated masculine paradigms. For more than twenty-five years, I have been writing and speaking about the changing roles of manhood, and I've noticed a shift in men's attitudes about this important topic. When I first began writing about men's issues back in the '90s, there were very few men talking about the challenges of being a man. Now, countless resources are available for any man who is courageous enough to embrace new ways of being and relating as men.

Truth be told, there are still very few men who are willing to engage in this new conversation about manhood. Most men are still extremely uncomfortable when it comes to discussing things like feelings, vulnerability, openness, sensitivity, and femininity. But since you're reading this book, I believe you are open and receptive to some new ideas about manhood and masculinity, and I can assure you your openness is the key to your happiness.

I want to share something I wrote that will serve as the foundation of this conversation. It's called the Rollercoaster, and it is a metaphor for society and how it impacts our lives as men.

The Rollercoaster

I had heard a lot about the rollercoaster. Initially, I didn't want to go and see it, but everyone kept saying, you have to check it out and get on it. It will be so much fun.

Reluctantly, I went to see it. It was intriguing and enticing, and it looked like fun.

You have to get on it, everyone said.

I'm not sure that I want to.

But everyone loves getting on the Rollercoaster, they said.

I don't think I'll like it.

Redefining Manhood and Masculinity

Go ahead and try it; you'll like it, everyone said.

So, I tried it.

In the beginning, it was fun. Going round and round and up and down with friends who also seemed to be having fun was initially enjoyable.

But after a short while, I got bored and tired. I didn't want to ride it anymore. I decided that I wanted to get off.

You can't get off, everyone said.

But I'm ready to.

No one gets off the rollercoaster once they get on.

Why not?

They just don't.

But I'm ready to get off.

Why not ride it a little longer and see if you'll change your mind? they said.

Okay, I'll try it a little longer. Round and round, up and down, I went pretending that I was enjoying myself.

But after a while, I began to get angry. I was tired of the rollercoaster, and I realized that I shouldn't have gotten on it in the first place. I wanted to get off, but I didn't know how.

I'm really sick of this rollercoaster. I want to get off right now.

We're sorry, but you must stay on the rollercoaster. That's the rule.

Well, I guess I'm going to have to break the rule because I'm about to get off.

But if you break the rule, no one will like you, and you will probably get hurt, they said.

I don't care about anyone else. I want to get off now. Who can I talk to about getting off this thing?

No one knows how to get off, they said.

I'm sure someone knows; I just have to find them.

It's been said that only a few people have ever gotten off this rollercoaster. And no one really knows what happened to them. Some believe that people have even been killed trying to get off. Why take that risk?

At this point, I'm willing to take that risk. I don't care what people think or what people are going to say. I refuse to keep going round and round and getting nowhere on this thing, and I must do something to get off.

I didn't know what to do, but I knew I couldn't stay on the rollercoaster. I needed a plan, and I needed it soon. I felt like I was dying and wanted to live again.

But what about the risk? What if what they say is true? What if I really can't get off or get killed trying to get off?

At this point, I decide that I have only one choice. And that choice is to live. I don't know what will happen, but I know I'm already dead if I stay on this thing. I have to trust my instincts, take the chance, and simply jump off. I'm not sure where I'll land or if I'll get hurt or even die, but I just know that I have to jump.

So despite what everyone else was saying and the fear and uncertainty I felt, I took a deep breath and jumped. As my body was hurled through the air uncontrollably, surprisingly, I felt a deep sense of calm and inner peace, and then I did exactly what I intuitively knew I could do - I flew!

So, can you relate to the story? Have you ever felt as if you were trapped on a rollercoaster and couldn't get off? Let's break down the story and better understand how human conditioning and programming work.

At the beginning of the story, I was paying more attention to what other people were saying instead of trusting my own instincts about the rollercoaster. Like too many people, we get tangled up in peer pressure and pay more attention to what others think and say than listening to our own inner voices. When I decided to get off, I was initially more concerned with what other people would say and think, and that's why I stayed on the rollercoaster longer than I wanted to.

It wasn't until I got bored and angry that I began to gain the courage to go against what everyone else was doing and saying. Once the boredom and pain became too great, I made a simple choice. I let go of my need to meet other people's approval and trusted my gut to do what was right for me. At that point, I was willing to accept the consequences of my choices and trusted my heart to make the choice to jump. Fear of jumping into the great unknown keeps most people trapped in lives of mediocrity and discontent.

The driving factor is fear. We are afraid of the unknown and uncertainty; for some people, it feels safer to just stay on the rollercoaster and do what everyone else is doing. By trusting my inner wisdom and letting go of the need to meet other people's approval, I embraced my fears and moved through them. Once I did this, I experienced true internal freedom, which allowed me to fly away and become the man I knew I could be.

This poem serves as the perfect metaphor for society. Most people are trapped on the rollercoaster and have no idea how to get off. I think most people don't want to get off because it's comfortable, and most people do not like being uncomfortable. If you're reading these words right now, I will assume you are one of the courageous ones willing to jump and be uncomfortable, so let's jump off and dive right in and get you off the rollercoaster.

Redefining Manhood and Masculinity

After my divorce, I had a burning desire to answer this question: What does it mean to be a man? I asked myself that question because I had done everything society says a man was supposed to do to be happy, but I was absolutely miserable. I was trapped on the societal rollercoaster, which said to be a man, you must have a wife, a house, 2.5 kids, 401k and vacations, and you will be happy. I had accomplished all of these things, but I definitely didn't feel happy.

I had fallen into a deep state of depression and had even considered taking my own life. After losing everything through divorce, bankruptcy, and foreclosure, I concluded that I really didn't have anything to live for.

But during the darkest period of my life, I received a miracle. I was sitting up late one night because I was too depressed to sleep. I was sitting at the edge of my bed, staring across the room at my bookshelf when I noticed every book on my bookshelf had something to do with getting rich or making money. As I sat there staring at the books, this question just popped into my head: "Michael, what if you took all of the energy you've used in trying to get rich and used that same energy to figure out how to be happy?"

It would be impossible for me to explain what happened in words, but suddenly, something in me shifted. All of a sudden, my depression lifted and I had this amazing clarity that I would be able to rebuild my life and it would become extraordinary.

The Brothahood of Kings

As a result of asking myself that question, I stopped reading books on getting rich and making money, and I began reading books on psychology, philosophy, metaphysics, and personal development.

I began what I'll call my journey of transformation. My journey led me to read hundreds of books, attend personal development seminars, listen to motivational audio programs, and begin a meditation practice.

As a result of my transformational journey, I was able to rebuild my life, and I can honestly say that at this very moment, I am happier than I have ever been. I have been happily married for almost 22 years, I am in great health, I get to do what I love to do: write books and give speeches, and I have a deep spiritual connection that nurtures my soul and gives me inner peace that defies description.

I share that story because I believe if you are reading this book right now, you can do the same thing. It is absolutely possible for you to have inner peace, dynamic health, great relationships, and financial abundance. You can definitely create the life of your dreams; it all begins with your willingness to jump off the rollercoaster and create the life you know you deserve.

So, are you willing to jump?

If you've gotten this far in the book, I believe the answer is yes, so let's jump off the rollercoaster and into your joy-filled life. But remember, it takes tremendous courage, commitment, perseverance, and patience. But rest assured, you have all of this inside of you already, so the only thing you must do now is make a commitment to yourself that you're ready to begin your transformational journey.

Since this chapter focuses on manhood and masculinity, I'd like to share something I wrote in my book, *A New Conversation With Men*. This will set the context for this chapter and provide some fuel for contemplation about what it means to be a man.

It is my fervent belief that men are frustrated, tired, and hungry. They are frustrated because they are trapped in an old paradigm that no longer works. They are frustrated because they are searching for new and better ways to exist as a man, yet they have failed in this search. They don't know where to turn and are becoming desperate for a new way of being and relating as a man.

They are tired of watching their families fall apart, their health deteriorate, and their wallets are emptied by divorce, materialism, and senseless addictions that rob them of not only their money but their self-esteem and dignity as well. They are tired of working at jobs that they hate just to try to keep up with the Joneses. They are tired of the emptiness and feeling of meaninglessness in their soul that tells them that there has to be another way to exist, yet they don't know how to change.

The Brothahood of Kings

They are hungry for something new and different, and I believe that something different is A New Conversation with Men.

I know this because I used to be one of those men. I know what it's like to be frustrated, tired, and hungry, and for the last twenty-five years, I have been removing this frustration, eliminating my exhaustion, and satisfying my hunger to become a better man. As a result, I will admit that my life is now working, and I feel happy and blessed to be a man. I wanted to share my story in hopes of empowering you to follow in my footsteps. I simply want you to become a better man.

This book is written to assist any man who wants to do just that: become a better man. It is written for the man who is sick and tired of being sick and tired, and it is written for that courageous man who refuses to settle for mediocrity and wants to live a life of excellence.

It's been said that, "There is no power in the universe that can stop an idea whose time has come." I believe the time has come for A New Conversation with Men, and there is nothing that can stop it. This book is written to start a new revolution for the hearts, minds, and souls of men everywhere, and my hope is that this revolution changes the world for the better.

Can you relate to this? Have you ever felt tired, frustrated, and hungry as a man?

Redefining Manhood and Masculinity

If the answer is yes, I will assert that you feel that way because you are trapped on the societal rollercoaster. The question now becomes, are you ready to get off?

If you pay attention to mainstream media, you may have concluded that men are the bad guys. We are constantly bombarded with stories of senseless acts of violence, infidelity, domestic abuse, fatherlessness, addictions, and corporate corruption. The truth of the matter is that men are not the problem; the problem is men are trapped in an antiquated paradigm of masculinity. In other words, they are trapped on the rollercoaster.

For example, for the past few years, one of the buzz words which has been getting a lot of coverage in the news is the term "toxic masculinity." Reporters use this term when they report on any story of a man doing "bad" things. The fact is there really is no such thing as toxic masculinity. Masculinity isn't toxic. When you see a man acting out negatively, that is toxic behavior, not toxic masculinity. I would suggest that a man acts out in a toxic way because he is disconnected from his authentic masculinity. Men who are connected to their authentic masculinity never act out in toxic ways.

Here is a simple way to understand masculinity.

Masculinity is simply an energy. Men have masculine energy, and women have masculine energy. Masculinity can be looked at as the energy of "Doing." On the other hand, there is feminine energy. Women have feminine energy and men have feminine energy. Femininity is the energy of "Being."

Neither one of these are toxic. Here are some traits of masculine energy.

Left brain focused, logical thinking, always doing, thinking, being disciplined, assertive, analytical, and aggressive.

Here are some traits of feminine energy.

Right brain focused, intuitive, feeling, creative, empathic, caring, knowing, and compassionate.

As mentioned, men and women both share these two energies. When we see men or women acting out in "toxic" ways, it is because they have been wounded in some way, and that is what causes them to do things we may consider toxic behaviors.

As a result of the research and studying I've done over the past twenty years, I have concluded there are five illusions of manhood that cause a man to act out in toxic ways. These illusions are perpetuated through our families, our cultures, and our media. In other words, these illusions are actually an integral aspect of being stuck on the rollercoaster. To break free from these illusions, a man must first become aware they even exist. So, I would like to share those five illusions with you now:

To be a man, you must be non-emotional and disconnected.

To be a man, you must use sexual conquest as a gauge for manhood.

To be a man, you must have money and material possessions.

To be a man, you must have status, positions, and power.

To be a man, you must win at all costs and compete against other men.

These five illusions are the foundation of all pain and misery in a man's life. If you will take a moment and really examine them, I believe you will see what I mean. To give you a better understanding of how these illusions affect your life I will now break them down and explain each one individually.

Illusion 1.

To be a man, you must be non-emotional and disconnected.

I believe this is the greatest illusion. All other illusions are actually built on top of this one. In our society, males are conditioned from a very young age not to feel. We are given the message that to feel and express those feelings is somehow weak or, worse, feminine. Therefore, we start accepting this illusion even as little boys. Think about the powerful messages you received as a young boy, things like, "Big boys don't cry," "Stop being a baby," and "Don't act like a sissy" are the beginning of the acceptance of this illusion. What actually occurs is we begin to shut down our emotions, and the only way to cope is to express ourselves through our intellect. We stop expressing how we feel and begin expressing what we think. Of course, there is absolutely nothing wrong with thinking. Using our intellect is an integral and necessary aspect of our humanity. Still, without our emotions, we become empty, hollow automatons that miss out on the most important aspect of our lives.

This illusion is powerful because, as men, we accept that the only appropriate feelings we should express are the negative ones. It's absolutely acceptable for a man to express anger and rage in our society without being accused of being less than a man, but if a man expresses joy, sadness, or fear, then his masculinity will always be questioned. A good example of this is a television interview back in 2008 with Terrell Owens, who was a wide receiver for the Dallas Cowboys football team. After the Cowboys suffered an emotional loss to the New York Giants, Terrell was defending his friend and quarterback Tony Romo. In the interview, Terrell began to cry as he openly shared how unfair the media was to his friend. It was obvious that the loss deeply saddened him, but he was also saying just how much he cared for his friend. As a result of this interview, his masculinity was immediately challenged. The media went into a frenzy about Terrell's emotional interview. Some sportscasters accused him of being weak and overly sensitive, while others even questioned his sexuality by implying that he might be gay.

The question I pose is, why is it so unacceptable in our society for a man to be emotional? Does it really make us less than men if we are comfortable expressing our feelings and wearing our hearts on our sleeves? Who decided that women could be emotional but not men?

This is accepted in our society because we are trapped in the illusion that men are supposed to be non-emotional and disconnected. It is an illusion that has been passed down for generations, and the time has come for us to wake up from this illusion. When a man is trapped in this illusion, he loses his ability to truly experience life as it was meant to. Without his emotions, he will miss out on the most important aspects of his life. His joy, passion, creativity, intuition, connection with his spouse and children, and even his faith are all connected to his ability to feel. So, it is important that we break free from this illusion and create a new paradigm in which men are comfortable expressing their emotions openly and honestly without fear of having our masculinity challenged.

Illusion 2.

To be a man, you must use sexual conquest as a gauge for manhood.

If you get nothing else from this book, I hope you will get this. This is one of the most destructive illusions perpetuated throughout our society. This illusion contributes to teenage pregnancy, divorce, rape, sexually transmitted diseases, and all sorts of violence. I cannot pinpoint when this illusion began, but I would assume it has been around since the beginning of time. It really doesn't matter when it started; the question we must ask ourselves is how can we end it?

Think back to your youth and see if you remember how prevalent this illusion was, especially during your younger days. Do you remember when you were young and the only thing you thought about was sex? As a teenager, our minds and our hormones were obsessed with the prospect of having sex. If we are honest with ourselves, we should recognize that almost everything we did somehow led to us trying to attract the opposite sex so that we could engage in the act of sex. We bought our cars to try to attract girls. We played sports hoping that it would attract girls. We bought clothes and kept our hair perfect in hopes of attracting girls. We made money to impress and attract girls. So why were we so obsessed with girls? Because we wanted to have sex! We all believed that by having sex, we would validate our manhood, our friends would cheer for us, and we would be happy and fulfilled. So if we weren't having sex, we usually lied about it just to make sure we maintained the illusion that we were real men. If we weren't having sex and maintaining this illusion, we usually felt inadequate and inferior as young men.

Now I would like you to fast forward to the present. If you will take a moment and ask yourself the same questions, you will see that most of us as men are still trapped in the same illusion. We buy cars to attract women. We play sports to attract women. We buy clothes and keep our hair perfect to attract women. We make money and spend money to attract and impress women. So why are we so obsessed with attracting women? Because we want to have sex with women!

And when we aren't having sex with women, we usually lie to our friends about it. Can you see the insanity in this? Sexual conquest does not make you a man. It is only an illusion and a temporary fix to your unhappiness. If you are using sex as a gauge for manhood, you are trapped in a vicious cycle of addiction and denial.

Illusion 3.

To be a man, you must have money and material possessions.

This illusion is the reason men spend billions upon billions of dollars buying "stuff." Too many of us believe that if we buy the right house, car, watch, or clothes, we will be viewed as men, and we will gain approval from our friends. This is the reason so many of us feel empty and discontented because we have bought into the illusion that if we accumulate enough "stuff," we will feel fulfilled. Nothing could be further from the truth. This illusion is why many of us try to "Keep up with the Joneses."

The Brothahood of Kings

As I think about this illusion, I'm reminded of my high school days when I purchased my first car. My first car was a 1969 Ford Mustang that I absolutely loved. But it wasn't the freedom that came from owning my own car that excited me; it was the fact that I had now become a man in my mind. Of course, I was only seventeen at the time and still living at home, but in my mind, I had graduated from adolescence and moved into manhood. (This just shows you how this particular illusion kicks in around our formative high school years.)

Another way that I bought into this illusion was by pretending that I had lots of money even when I didn't. I remember keeping a big wad of cash in my pocket at all times, and I would always have a twenty or fifty-dollar bill on top with lots of one-dollar bills on the bottom. Whenever I would be out with my friends, I would pull out my wad of cash and pretend that I had a lot more money than I actually did. Since most of my friends didn't have jobs or money, I was always seen as "The Man" by my peers. This was definitely a big boost for my ego, but it caused me to fall deeper and deeper into the illusion.

These are just two examples of the things some of us as men do when we are trapped in this illusion. Sadly, there are currently lots of men out there today who are still doing the things that I did in high school. (Are you one of them?) They are the ones who have become trapped in the illusion that they must have money and material things to be a man, and I can assure you that they are paying a significant price in terms of their emotional, psychological, and spiritual well-being.

Illusion 4.

To be a man, you must have status, positions, and power.

Have you ever noticed how our society adores celebrities, sports figures, and executives? We are taught that, "He who has the gold makes the rules," which implies that the more money you have, the "better" you are as a person. The implication is that somehow men who are wealthier or have higher societal status are somehow "superior" to other men. This is definitely an illusion. The truth is that monetary wealth does not make you a better man. It may make your life easier, but it does not make a man superior to other men. The sad part is that too many men accept this illusion and spend all of their energy trying to move up the societal ladder to validate themselves. They invest all of their time and energy in trying to gain titles and labels, while in reality, they feel empty and unfulfilled. They try to compensate for this emptiness by acting "superior" even though they really aren't.

I must admit that I was definitely caught in this illusion several years ago. Although I did not consider myself superior to any other man, I believed that attaining the title of "Manager" would somehow validate me as a man. Although I did not recognize it at the time, my ambition and drive were fueled by my insecurities about being a man. In my mind, climbing the corporate ladder and becoming successful was a way to prove to myself that I was competent and intelligent. Unfortunately, even after I made it to the top, I still felt the same insecurities. Even though I put up the facade of being in control and in charge, a part of me was a frightened little boy simply trying to find his way home.

Too many men are currently caught in this illusion of manhood. You can recognize them by their big egos and their arrogance. They parade around town flashing their titles at you and trying to get the external validation they desperately need. On the outside, they may appear to have it all together, but on the inside, they are wounded little boys doing their best to maintain their charade.

Illusion 5.

To be a man, you must win at all costs and compete against other men.

This is probably the least recognized of all the illusions. Although we seldom talk openly about this, an unspoken male law says that we are supposed to always compete against each other. This can be witnessed on a large scale by corporate corruption. When a man's ego gets inflated, he will do anything to "stay on top." All rational thinking will go out the window if a man thinks his competitor is ahead of him. Our business schools would teach you that being competitive is the foundation of success. Still, they will not teach you about the consequences of this overly competitive, macho position that too many men fall victim to.

A perfect example of this on a small scale is my experience as a salesman in a hardware store. One day I sold a customer a very expensive bar-b-que grill. The customer wanted to make sure that it had all of the latest technology, and he wanted it to be the "best." I worked with him for a couple of days until I finally put together the grill of his dreams. As he walked out of the store, his final comment to me was, "Thanks for helping me put together such an awesome grill. My neighbor is going to be green with envy."

A couple of days later, a gentleman shows up and asks to speak to me about purchasing a grill. He specifically asked for me because his neighbor told him I was very helpful. He raved about how awesome his neighbor's grill was and said he wanted to purchase one just like it. But then he added that he wanted to ensure that it had at least one feature that his neighbor's grill did not have. He did not care what the feature was; as a matter of fact, he even mentioned that he probably wouldn't use the new feature. He simply wanted to make sure that it was better than his neighbor's grill.

This is what happens when you get caught in this illusion. You will do irrational things and then rationalize them by saying you work hard for your money and deserve the best.

Of course, there is nothing wrong with wanting the best for yourself, but when you get trapped in this illusion, you will ultimately experience emptiness.

These are the five illusions of manhood that are perpetuated throughout our society. It is absolutely imperative that you recognize these illusions and not be trapped by them. The intention of a new conversation with men is to assist you in breaking free from all of these illusions, so I would like to share some concrete things you can do to break free from the illusions.

1. **You must be willing to become aware that the illusion exists**

This is always the most difficult and challenging step, and at the same time, it is always the first step. As soon as you become aware that you are trapped in the illusion, you have already begun waking up from it. Take some time and reflect on these illusions and then write down the one that resonates the most for you. By writing down the illusion, it will begin to lose its grip on you. Imagine the illusion as internal darkness and your awareness as eternal light. By shining the light onto the darkness, the darkness disappears. Your awareness is the light that will remove the darkness. Challenge yourself to become aware of the illusion you may be caught in.

2. **You must be willing to be transformed by the renewing of your mind**

Redefining Manhood and Masculinity

This is what I mean by having a new conversation with men. It means becoming aware of old belief systems, thought patterns, and assumptions in your mind that may no longer work for you. By changing your internal dialog (conversation), you lay the foundation for new ways of being a man. Think of your mind as a garden and your thoughts as seeds. Whatever seed (thought) you plant has to grow. If you are planting negative seeds, guess what grows? If you are planting positive seeds, what do you think will sprout up? Transforming your mind means that you make a conscious effort to recognize what types of seeds you are planting. The more conscious you become, the more likely you are to plant positive seeds.

This also means that you become conscious of all the things you are allowing to be planted in your mind. This means that you should limit your exposure to all of the negative seeds planted by our media. So do yourself a favor and disconnect from too much television.

3. **You must be willing to heal and reconnect to your emotions**

This is definitely our greatest challenge as men. As I mentioned, we are conditioned not to feel, but it is our responsibility to go against societal conditioning and become courageous enough to begin our emotional healing process. Until you learn to heal and feel, something will always be missing in your life. I will go into greater depth and detail about this in an upcoming chapter.

4. You must seek support

You must understand that you cannot do this alone. I understand how difficult it is for men to seek support, but the fact remains you must seek help. I don't care if you go to therapy, join a men's group, join AA, or go to a church group. It is important that you surround yourself with like-minded men who can support and challenge you to become the best man you can be. Gaining the courage to seek support is a surefire way to help you break free from these illusions. I highly recommend that you join our online community at www.brothahoodofkings.com because it is filled with resources designed to help you break free from these illusions, and it will put you in contact with other men on the same journey as you. They can serve as role models and mentors and help you recognize that you are never alone.

5. You must develop a spiritual connection that works for you

This does not necessarily mean you have to join a church or other religious organization. It means that you must come to your own understanding that there is a power greater than yourself in the universe. By connecting to this power, it will give you strength, faith, and courage to break free from the illusions and live a more rewarding and fulfilling life. Once you develop this connection, it is your responsibility to nurture it and ensure that you stay connected to it.

Redefining Manhood and Masculinity

So there you have them, the five illusions of manhood:

1. To be a man, you must be non-emotional and disconnected.

2. To be a man, you must have status, positions, and power.

3. To be a man, you must have money and material possessions.

4. To be a man, you must use sexual conquest as a gauge for manhood.

5. To be a man, you must win at all costs and compete against other men.

And these are the five things you can do to wake up from the illusions:

1. You must be willing to become aware that the illusion exists.

2. You must be willing to be transformed by the renewing of your mind.

3. You must be willing to heal and reconnect to your emotions.

4. You must seek support.

5. You must develop a spiritual connection that works for you.

In order to make the world a better place, we must recognize these illusions and remove them from our collective psyches. It begins with each man waking up and choosing to break free from these illusions. In doing so, the world will be a much better place for everyone.

The Brothahood of Kings

Are you willing to look at the man in the mirror and ask him to change his ways?

This is the intention of the Brothahood of Kings movement. We are committed to empowering black men to embrace new ideas about manhood and masculinity that will support them in creating extraordinary lives. To do this, you must be willing to look at the man in the mirror and ask him to change his ways so he can become a better man.

Are you willing to become a better man?

"There have been many changes in the gender roles over the past 30 or more years. As a result, the idea of being a "real man" has changed but one thing is for sure — there are some traits that define masculinity that most men and women would still agree upon." -Unknown

Chapter 3

Zen and The Art of Mature Masculinity

By

Greg "Reimoku" Smith

"In becoming forcibly and essentially aware of my mortality, and of what I wished and wanted for my life, however short it might be, priorities and omissions became strongly etched in a merciless light, and what I most regretted were my silences. Of what had I *ever* been afraid?"

-Audrey Lorde (The Transformation of Silence into Language and Action)

Our Shining Opportunity

Leading Black feminist scholar, author, and Ancestor, Bell Hooks, in her seminal work, *The Will to Change: Men, Masculinity, and Love,* sounds the clarion call for the worldwide repudiation of patriarchal mores in favor of what she calls a 'love ethic.' She asserts that:

> "Patriarchy is the single most life-threatening disease…a [sociopolitical] system that insists that males are inherently dominating, superior to everything and everyone deemed weak, especially females, …endowed with the right to dominate and rule over the weak and to maintain that dominance through various forms of psychological terrorism and violence".

'Mores' refer to normative ways of thinking and behaving within a group that reflects its fundamental values. These include spoken and unspoken agreements that individuals abide by in order to reinforce the status quo and ideally ensure their survival. The ties that bind this group together and form its core identities often consist of shared behavioral codes that signify whether one is a part of the in-group or not. Furthermore, depending on the culture, the risks of challenging these social protocols could entail certain consequences, among them being expulsion from the group, violence, or even death. Ultimately, the benefits of subverting patriarchy, both within and without, far outweigh the risks.

While patriarchy and masculinity overlap considerably in many cultures around the world, healing from the wounds of the former requires that the two be made conceptually distinct. The primary constituents of patriarchal masculinity being called into disrepute are: "avoiding femininity, restrictive emotionality, seeking achievement and status, self-reliance, aggression, homophobia, and nonrelational attitudes toward sexuality". These social codes often go unquestioned and deny men access to "full emotional well-being," which ultimately robs them of their ability to love. From a sociological perspective, masculinity is a mosaic of inherited, sociocultural, behavioral patterns, codes, roles, rituals, states of mind, aesthetics, and values that tend to be ascribed to and inculcated into males. One can think of it more simply as "the mores of men." The same observation applies to femininity and females. Of course, it goes without saying that no particular sex, or person for that matter, holds a monopoly on masculinity or femininity.

Hooks goes further, explaining that beside the social disease of patriarchy stand the interlocking forces of white supremacy, imperialism, capitalism, and heteronormativity, which, to a great extent, have not only shaped American culture but also normative, male socialization. Consequently, undoing patriarchy is also intimately tied to dismantling and creating sustainable alternatives to the aforementioned socioeconomic and political systems. Much to Hooks' chagrin, "radical feminist critique of patriarchy has practically been silenced in our culture" and "become a subcultural discourse available only to well-educated elites". With that in mind, now is the time for men to reclaim the parts of our humanity that have been hidden, denied and repressed as a result of patriarchal socialization and to rekindle our innate capacity to live in integrity, connectedness, and love.

Our shining opportunity as men is that we are endowed with the capacity to create ourselves "as a work of art," to quote the French philosopher, Michel Foucault. In that same vein, we not only get to collectively undo the patriarchal conditioning that many of us have inherited but also dream up new 'masculinities' with a common love ethic at its core. According to Hooks, "a love ethic presupposes that everyone has the right to be free, to live fully and well…by…embracing a global vision wherein we see our lives and our fate as intimately connected to those of everyone else on the planet" (All About Love: New Vision, pp. 87-88). All human beings, especially men, stand to benefit from this critical paradigm shift from patriarchy to full-fledged personhood. Hooks urges the public to "reclaim feminism for men, showing why feminist thinking and practice are the only way we can truly address the crisis of masculinity today…Men cannot change if there are no blueprints for change. Men cannot love if they are not taught the art of loving" (2004, xvii). The work must start from within, and The Brothahood of Kings Collective (BKC) exists to do just that. Just like our founding organization, the Brothahood, our mission is to "co-create a world of emotionally attuned men, connected to their hearts, who are in alignment with their values of a just and fair society…[We] look inward and discover what is true for us and find the courage to make the choices that best serve our community." Indeed, we are the answer to Hooks' call for change.

Our Love Ethic

Our intergenerational fraternal society was born as a weekly, virtual gathering in which mostly Black and indigenous men could introspect and engage in civil discourse. The intention was to give those men who had less experience with personal development work a chance to stick their pinky toes in, so to speak. Skilled coaches facilitate these meetings and offer in-the-moment emotional intelligence techniques while making sure that the container stays as psychically safe as possible. What's more, each man gets the opportunity to explore his inner depths with no real-world consequences. He reflects on his choices, lifestyle, and conditioning, along with the impacts these may have on his life and the life of others. He is then championed to make new choices that align with who he says he wants to be. All of this takes place within a radically loving and connected environment wherein accountability and integrity act as cardinal virtues. The goal is to resocialize ourselves into a deeper understanding of what it means to embody the mature masculine. This, however, is just the beginning.

Zen and The Art of Mature Masculinity

In my mind's eye, I see BKC as the preeminent model of mature masculinities that are elevated to the status of a fine art. One might even call it a masculine liberationist movement. Through initiation rituals, personal development and educational initiatives, as well as intergenerational mentorship, BKC reimagines masculinity as a prosocial art form that becomes a transmittable ethos for the benefit of posterity. To put it more simply, it is a Way of Being, much like the concept of the Tao and Yin and Yang in many Eastern philosophies. It is a non-dualistic concept that must recognize its counterpart, the feminine, as an integral part of itself in order to exist and flourish. To deny this principle is tantamount to rejecting oneself and inevitably leads to not only self-sabotage but self-destruction as well. One need not look further than the way that patriarchy, which is simply the masculine principle taken to its extreme, has manifested as the socioeconomic system of capitalism. For the sake of clarity, when I say "capitalism," I am not referring to the free market and the ability to exchange goods and services as one pleases. Instead, I am calling out business models that center on profit as their *sole* indicator of wealth and progress. By extension, men who have internalized the fickle promises of rampant capitalism often conflate their wealth and worth. This could not be further from the truth. It comes as no surprise, then, that any identity structure, namely patriarchal masculinity, that is founded upon instability is destined for a recession.

Consequently, much of the work that takes place within men's personal development circles entails combing through the tangled web of deeply internalized shaming messages that arise as a result of believing they have somehow failed to measure up to the patriarchal ideal. I am here to tell you that that ideal was not created with us men in mind. It is rather the unfortunate carryover of an intensely depersonalizing process through which men are resocialized into soldiers. Men who do not think or feel are the greatest assets of an imperialist regime, for they will jump at its beck and call. They will be able to take life at the bark of a command with no time or space to process the ensuing cascade of shame and guilt. Along with the creation of a mature masculine ideal, we also get the opportunity to recreate the warrior archetype, which focuses on connecting with and disciplining our primal instincts. Naturally, respect for all beings and protecting life are central to this ethos.

On another note, while there are numerous, personal reasons as to why many male, queer folks disidentify with manhood and masculine identity, my experience has led me to believe that it has to do, in large part, with their reckoning with the ills of patriarchal masculinity. This does not mesh with how they see themselves, or with how they wish to see the world. The cognitive dissonance produced between who they were taught to be and who they are makes it easier to discard the identity altogether and start anew, rather than salvage the old one. The big picture here is the radical notion that the mature masculine assumes responsibility for the state of society as a reflection of his own consciousness. Truth be told, disillusionment is a necessary and sacred part of awakening. BKC exists to hold and nurture men through this scary process of creating new standards of wealth and worth, ones that are just as personal as they are collective.

Mature masculinity can thus be conceptualized as a simultaneously deconstructive and constructive process whereby new, identity-shaping, internal dialogues are co-created about what it means to be a man. No man tells another what that is; he must discover it for himself. BKC does provide blueprints he can follow, however. Men do their inner work vicariously by witnessing that of other men or directly through their own introspection. Also, the concept of the mature masculine can take numerous forms: a process, a path, a principle, a contemplative discipline, a craft, an ethic, and an aesthetic. It defies the limits of rigid, gendered categorization and demands both wholehearted study and rigorous moral application. The foundational principles of the BKC love ethic, as I see them, reflect the quintessential paradigmatic shifts from dysfunctional, patriarchal masculinity to mature masculine ethos. Because volumes could be written about all of these concepts, I will offer concise definitions of each below.

FROM	TO
1. Domination →	1. S.O.U.L.
2. Aggression →	2. Wise Force
3. Avoiding Femininity →	3. Psychospiritual Wholeness
4. Restrictive Emotionality →	4. Emotional Artistry
5. Seeking achievement and status →	5. Living Ancestorhood
6. Self-reliance →	6. Interbeing
7. Otherphobia →	7. Ubuntu
8. Non-relational attitudes toward sexuality →	8. C.O.N.S.E.N.T.

1. **S.O.U.L. - Synergistic, Service-Oriented, Upstanding Leadership** - a humane, cooperative style of directing a harmonized unit, wherein the leader participates as part of the group, ethically models expected performance, genuinely cares for everyone, nurtures their respective skill sets, and implements a co-created mission that serves to improve the state of humanity.

2. **Wise Force** - skillfully harnessed primal energy that is exercised with the utmost care and discernment in such a way that is wholly appropriate to the circumstances and minimizes harm as much as reasonably possible.

3. **Psychospiritual Wholeness** - having access to both masculine and feminine energies within.

4. **Emotional Artistry** - the polished application of emotionally intelligent virtues and the ability to navigate life with confidence, charisma, curiosity, creativity, finesse, and humor.

5. **Living Ancestorhood** - seeing oneself as a parent to future generations and passing down wealth, resources, and blueprints for life that will maximize their well-being.

6. **Interbeing** - recognizing one's existence as intimately interdependent with all others and the willingness to both offer and accept help and support.

7. **Ubuntu** - a word existing within the Bantu language family that expresses the worldview, "I am because we are"

8. **C.O.N.S.E.N.T. - Choosing Open-hearted, Non-violent, Safe Expressions of Natural Tendencies** - asking for and receiving unmistakably clear permission to engage in intimate or sexual acts with another person(s).

Our Cardinal Virtues

This list would not be complete without the following virtues that serve as the backbone of men's personal development work:

1. **Courage** - the "mother of all virtues" - the willingness to respond dutifully to fear.

2. **Unconditional Self-Love and Acceptance** - treating and speaking to oneself kindly and gently.

3. **Universal Compassion** - the desire for all beings to be happy and free.

4. **Integrity** - the alignment of words and actions.

5. **Accountability** - telling on oneself and making amends for broken agreements.

Our Destiny

I envision a world of joyful men who are enraptured by the Spirit and overcome with a fundamental exultation for life. I envision a world of men who choose to unconditionally love and accept themselves, especially in the midst of hard times. I envision a world of emotionally intelligent representatives of the mature masculine who have the tools to navigate life with confidence. I envision a world whose generations of men are radically well, who live long, healthy lives, have access to quality education, and create reliable streams of income. I envision a world in which men are empowered to participate fully in life and foster societal change by always giving precedence to "nonviolent action over violence, peace over war, life over death" (2004, 118). Indeed, these men prioritize what they want to live for over what they want to die for. I envision a world of open-hearted men who express their feelings, honor their word and treat the feminine, both within and without, as sacred. I envision a world of men who are deeply connected to a sense of mission and purpose and direct their lives accordingly. I envision a world of men who cherish and protect the Earth, just as they would their own bodies. I envision a world of men who are able to engage in civil discourse and have the flexibility of mind to find value in different beliefs, experiences, and lifestyles. These men possess the wisdom to see all challenges as opportunities for growth and the courage to surmount them with grace, creativity and humor. I envision a world of men who see every thought and action as a prayer decreed and who possess an unshakeable inner knowing of the Great I Am. I envision a world of men who unlock the great gifts and magic held within their body-temple and experience how good it is meant to feel. I envision a world of men who openly and unapologetically share physical affection and tenderness with one another. I envision a world of men who are attuned to their inner child, never losing sight of their own innocence, play, and infinite curiosity. I envision a world of men who integrate their shadows and recognize them as a part of their innate wholeness. I envision a world in which highly sensitive men, like me, are valued for their unique gifts, honored for their rich inner life, and assume their rightful place as the conscientious, priestly advisors of society. Yes, this vision is alive within me! It vibrates in the marrow of my bones! This truth rings clear in my gut. This is why I am here. I surrender to the momentous current that sees me to the end. And so it is!

"There are wounds that never show on the body that are deeper and more hurtful than anything that bleeds."
– Laurell K. Hamilton

Chapter 4

A Brotha's Trauma

By

Paul Randolph Newell

Brother, we all have trauma. Personally, I never wanted to believe that I had traumas, and once I did, my perceptions and behaviors shifted, and I gained a higher sense of self that I had been seeking for a while. First, I'll admit I failed to really know trauma, what it can look like, and the areas of life it can impact. By definition, trauma is a distressing or disturbing experience, and the experience can spark an emotional shock that can lead to long-term conditions like depression, anxiety, and addictions.

Experiencing a traumatic event can harm a person's sense of safety, sense of self, and ability to regulate emotions and navigate relationships. When I looked deeper into the word, it led me to its Greek origin meaning, "wound." The wounds of trauma are invisible to the human eye yet anchored in our souls.

As a Man of Color (MOC), I realized in my older years the impact trauma has had on my life and the endurance and skills I've developed in masking it. Well, at least, THINKING I was masking it.

After years of therapy, Men's work, and doing my own self work to explore my stories and patterns, I concluded that I had developed a high threshold for trauma. I originally thought trauma had to be something severe like an accident or physical and/or emotional abuse. I learned that traumas could be more subtle, which became evident after my divorce. If you are reading this and have been divorced, you may relate to the devastation that can cause in your relationship with yourself and others, especially if kids are involved.

When I experienced divorce and all the extras that came with it, I was in a dark and low place. I would mainly feel anger, sadness, humiliation, and powerlessness. What I felt sparked behaviors that led me into an even deeper and darker hole that led to more life twists in the form of fathering two additional children with two different women. All this was happening while I was going back and forth to court, fielding constant emails and phone calls from my divorce lawyer, and keeping my shit together while working a full-time job to provide for bills, my apartment, and half the mortgage on a house I wasn't living in.

Even as I write this, I recall this stage of my life and wonder how I got through it. Oh, I know how I got through it; I drank, I smoked, I sexed, and I did whatever else I could get myself into to escape the pain I was in and avoid the life I was living.

After doing my work and finally getting curious about my behaviors and patterns, I realized the life I was living resulted from trauma in three major areas: My childhood, My relationships, and My race.

The revealing of my trauma in these areas reared its ugly head in three distinct situations in my life, and I'm ready to share them with you. My intention is that my words will open the door for you to address any traumas you may have experienced for you to live your life on a top-notch level.

Okay, let's dive into these experiences. And please note: the work I've done to address my trauma continues to this day and has become more of a practice. There are some questions I resort to when I experience an activation of my trauma. I'll share those with you as well.

The Household Splits When I was five, my parents separated and started their divorce process. Looking back on this time, I failed to remember the details of being at our old house (old house referring to the house my whole family lived in).

After therapy and mentoring in the Omega Point Program, I was able to unearth memories of my time at our old house. Those memories were graphic and violent; in those memories, I felt the sadness, fear, and chaos alive and well within and around our family. As I unearthed my experiences, they explained the traumas that impacted me later in life. I began to remember the aggression and volatility and realized how I turned off memories to protect myself. I splintered off parts of myself with each perceived traumatic event. While there was violence in our household, my perception of abandonment ended up having the biggest impact on me. I perceived that the family unit was being abandoned because of me and that I was the cause of this separation.

The weight of guilt and thinking I destroyed my family was an emotional trauma that brought pain and dis-ease.

The Black Spectrum: Growing up in a predominantly affluent white town was another trauma that lasted with me and impacted how I lived life. My parents moved from Jamaica to New Jersey so our family would be raised in an area of opportunity. In our house, we were trained to speak properly, dress well, be articulate, and be obedient. All these things sound great, right? Well, they had their gifts and their curses. I created personas to establish safety, to be liked, and accepted, and this started in my younger years when I was in elementary school.

I was one of the few black kids, and looking back on it, I now know that I experienced microaggressions in statements like, "you dress so well," "you speak so well," and at the time, I thought of them as compliments. On the opposite side, the other kids of color failed to accept me. They thought I acted white and was a sell-out. I wasn't accepted, and I wanted to be because I looked like them, they looked like me, and that was a sad space to be in because I had nowhere to turn, and this is when I began to isolate myself.

It became more comfortable for me to go inside and be by myself rather than to stay outside and learn what it means to trust people who look like me and those who don't. The experience that I got from the other kids was a form of bullying, and while it was far from painful physically, it left a wound emotionally and spiritually. The wounds breed a people pleaser, a captain save-a-hoe, and a passive-aggressive male.

The Trials of Leaving When I made a choice to leave my marriage and family, it was a difficult decision that started activating the trauma of putting my son in the type of chaos that I grew up in. While it was a difficult decision to make, I knew at the time I had to leave or else I would end up killing myself or killing her. The divorce process activated many emotions like anger, sadness, grief, guilt, and shame. Add to that the powerlessness I felt in family court, the financial stress, and processing grief of my mom passing.

As a man of color, my experience in those courts revealed deep wounds of segregation, slavery, and buck-breaking, and I found myself covering up and hiding what I was experiencing. Doing that actually created a space for me to breed anxiety and depression, which led back to more drinking, smoking, and engaging in unprotected sex (resulting in fathering two more children with two different women).

The Traumas: In my shared experiences above, I claimed certain traumas I recognized from those situations. Acknowledging the trauma supported me in overcoming them. Let's take a moment to identify different types of trauma. Please note: I am far from an expert on these things. I'm sharing this from my perspective, research, and education.

Chronic trauma is repeated and prolonged exposure to highly stressful events. Early childhood trauma occurs when a person between birth and the age of six witnesses or experiences overwhelming negative events or continued exposure to abuse, assault, neglect, violence, exploitation, or bullying. We are all born with an energy system, also known as the chakra system.

The root portion or our energy system is developed between the ages of zero and eight; during that time, each person develops their sense of self. This root is the seat of our stability and sense of security and is the beginning of us learning what it means to be safe. Complex trauma is exposure to varied and multiple traumatic events, often of an invasive, interpersonal nature, often occurring in childhood, which disrupts many aspects of development and one's sense of self.

Emotional/psychological trauma results from an extremely stressful event that causes severe disability in daily functioning. This may include events such as a physical assault, emotional or verbal abuse, a life-threatening medical condition, an act of terror, or a natural disaster.

As I listed out the traumas from my experiences, I noticed they are all interpersonal trauma, meaning trauma that happens between people. Acknowledging this opened up my perceptions of my past and current experiences and exposed the symptoms of post-traumatic stress that I was living through in different areas of my life. Those symptoms were: feelings of worthlessness, shame, and guilt - my feelings as a Father and as a man. I was struggling and often thought of killing myself because I thought everyone would be better off without me.

Problems controlling your emotions - heavily relying on vices to main emotional balance and wearing a mask and pretending to be having a good time when I was really masking my loneliness and despair. I was finding it hard to feel connected with others -I isolated often and wore multiple masks to hide what was happening. I never wanted anyone to know what I was going through with relationship problems, like having trouble keeping friends and partners, fathering two children with two different women, and creating disconnection with my first son—looking for love in all the wrong places. As my symptoms became clearer, I acknowledged my high trauma threshold.

Our Trauma Threshold: A threshold is a level or point at which you start to experience something or at which something starts to happen. As a people, we have a high threshold for trauma. As I think about that, I believe it's due to our environment, the things that we see in our communities. The violence and degradation become normal and commonplace to the point that our experiences are gaslit and discounted. We see people that look like us beaten and murdered in life, film, music, and media. And in all that, a part of us becomes conditioned to believing that's the way it is and has been.

This unconscious and insidious mindset endure trauma because it appears normal to us. The barrage of images bombarding our conscious and subconscious reactivate wounds from those that came before us. The concept of epigenetics talks about the fact that our DNA has lived for generations before and will go on for generations after. Epigenetic research has found that trauma, survival tactics, and patterns can be passed on between generations. What does that mean, and what does that have to do with trauma? It is connected because the trauma and the horrific experiences that our ancestors experienced are carried on in us and can easily be activated.

While we as a culture will acknowledge the travesties that have occurred against people of color, we as a culture also pride ourselves on being resilient and on being stronger than our situations in life. My personal research on trauma led me to Evette Rose, an Author, Life Coach, and Founder of Metaphysical Anatomy. She explains that trauma is free of making anyone stronger and someone can be desensitized and able to suppress past trauma.

In our communities, our perception of strength may actually be an ability to collectively dissociate, avoid, and numb ourselves. I learned from reading Evette's book and my personal journey that numbing my traumas allowed them to fester inside until another trauma showed up and added to what I was already holding.

Here's science on this from some research done by Author and Neuroscientist Dr. Robert C. Scaer. Dr. Scaer found that humans can physically survive trauma, yet a human never completes a trauma cycle. The traumatic experience may be imprinted and stored in the brain or body. When humans fail to release, they carry that trauma for life. Evette calls this surviving trauma rather than completing drama.

Trauma to Triumph: My People, it's time… it's our time to embrace and address those experiences that happened to us to speak on them and be free of reliving them as a victim. It's more of reliving them from a different perspective to see the impacts that experience is having on my life now. What were the patterns, the stories, and the behaviors that I started to adopt and adapt to survive this trauma rather than address it?

So here are some things as you're reading this information. If you're experiencing trauma, the key thing to do is to see a professional to support you in moving through this. This could be a therapist or an energy worker; this could be someone that was experienced in moving through intense traumas. The trauma can be intense when you finally uncover it, and it could be devastating too when one understands the impact that trauma has had, and I'm speaking from experience.

Something that helped me along with therapy and coaching was doing my inner work to address my traumas from a bigger and higher perspective. To do this, I got to look back at my traumas and envision myself as the hero coming into a scenario to "save" me. This exercise took a willingness to step into my imagination to address parts of myself that I separated from because of traumas.

When I was in therapy last year, I remembered a traumatic scenario in my life that provided space for me to complete my trauma. In that scenario, the first question I asked myself was, "Who or what needs protecting in this scenario?" Then after I acknowledge the answer to that question, I become a wise hero who will protect what or who needs protecting. And the question that activates that part of me is, "How will I protect?" That question is where the magic happens for me because in answering that question of myself, I begin extracting the support I did need and want in those scenarios that I failed to get. And because I failed to get what I needed in my younger years, I lived my life from trauma and I found myself completely numbing myself out to my pains and vices.

This activity always reminds me that the only one that can ever save you is you, and my hope is that this book provides you with some insights to help you heal your trauma, so you become emotionally., psychologically, and spiritually free.

"Until you heal the wounds of your past, you are going to bleed. You can bandage the bleeding with food, with alcohol, with drugs, with work, with cigarettes, with sex, but eventually, it will all ooze through and stain your life. You must find the strength to open the wounds, stick your hands inside, pull out the core of the pain that is holding you in your past, the memories, and make peace with them."
- Iyanla Vanzant

Chapter 5

You Must Make Peace With Your Past

When I became involved with personal development programs in 1990, I was really drawn to the teaching of the power of positive thinking. I had always been optimistic, so it was a natural progression for me to really embrace what many motivational speakers were preaching. Their message was always to be positive and look at the bright side of things. This positive thinking allowed me to deal with the multiplicity of challenges I was dealing with at the time. If not for my positive thinking, I'm sure that I would have fallen into a deep abyss of despair and depression, which may have ultimately ended in my demise.

But I embraced the positive thinking mantra and committed to always thinking positively. Without question, this way of thinking has positively impacted my life. Still, there is a negative side of positive thinking that I want to share, to shed some light on why positive thinking sometimes doesn't work and can also be detrimental to your life.

The biggest lesson I learned about the detrimental effects of positive thinking occurred while I was basically homeless. I had a friend who allowed me to stay at her house for a while until I could find my own place. During that time, I searched for employment and did everything I could to get back on my feet. I didn't own a car, and she sometimes let me borrow hers to look for employment. She was an absolute angel to whom I am forever indebted for her generosity, caring, and friendship.

One evening my friend came home and asked me how my day went. I told her about the rejections I had received while trying to find a job, and I told her that I was still optimistic that I would find a job soon.

She then looked at me with a caring, compassionate heart and asked how I was really doing. The conversation went something like this:

Her: *Michael, tell me how you're really doing. How are you feeling right now?*

Me: *I'm doing great! Although I didn't find a job, I'm confident that I will soon and I will be able to get back on my feet.*

Her: *But Michael, you didn't answer my question. How are you feeling right now? At this very moment, how do you feel?*

Me: *I told you I'm doing great. I know the Universe will support me and help me find a job, so I'm excited and happy about my future.*

Her: *Michael, I think that's bullshit! You keep saying you're doing great, but the truth is you aren't. Right now, your life is a mess, and you're unwilling to be completely honest with yourself about how you really feel. I believe in you and have faith that you will get your life on track, but until you can be completely honest with yourself about how you feel, not what you think, you won't be able to change. I personally think that you are in denial, and you are hiding behind your positive thinking and denying how you really feel. Can you tell me right now exactly what you're feeling?*

Me: *I told you, I'm doing great. I've got some challenges to deal with, but I keep telling you I'll deal with them. What more do you want me to say?*

Her: *I want you to share your feelings with me. Tell me what's going on inside you. Not what's in your head, but what's in your heart. How do you feel?*

Me: *I don't really understand what you're asking. I keep telling you that I'm fine. What else can I say?*

Her: *So Michael, answer this question, how does it make you feel not to be able to have your own home and have to rely on other people? Does it make you sad? Does it make you angry?*

You Must Make Peace With Your Past

How did you feel when you were rejected for the jobs you applied for today? Were you upset? Were you disappointed? Were you afraid?

Or how does it make you feel when you know you can't see your kids because you don't have transportation or money to visit them? Doesn't that make you feel sad?

Do you see what I mean now? I want you to share your emotions with me. I want you to express your feelings. Can you do that?

Me: *I'm not sure.*

Her: *Michael, you and I have been through a lot together as friends. I love how you are able to be optimistic, and I love how you can find the good in all situations. But the truth is that you aren't connected to your emotions and hide behind being positive and intellectual. You are so stuck in your head that you can't feel from your heart.*

You are my friend and I love you. I will never judge you or reject you. I'm not asking anything from you except your willingness to be authentic and real with me. Can you do that? Can you share yourself with me in that way?

After listening to her for a moment, I started to allow myself to feel. I started looking closer at myself for what emotions were present, and suddenly I knew what she meant. At that moment, I felt my heart begin to surrender, and I began to speak.

Me: I understand what you mean now. If I'm completely honest, I feel sad and afraid. I'm sad because I feel like less than a man because I have to rely on you to care for me. I feel afraid that I will not be able to find a job, and ultimately, you will have to kick me out on the streets, and I'm not sure what I will do.

Her: That's what I'm talking about. Keep sharing.

Tell me more about how you feel.

Me: I feel like a failure right now. I worked so hard to build my perfect life, only to have it come crashing down on me. I've lost everything. I lost my wife, my kids, my home, my job, and my self-esteem. I feel lonely and sad right now.

All of a sudden, my friend walked over and began to hug me. She took me in her arms and told me everything would be okay. She assured me that it is okay to share what I'm feeling and that it does not make me less of a man to do so. As she continued to hold me in her warm embrace, I continued to share how I was feeling. I allowed all the trapped emotions to come out, and the tears began to flow. I found myself releasing years of repressed pain, sadness, and disappointment, and the emotions just began to pour out of me through my tears. Although it was extremely painful, it was also therapeutic. Allowing myself to feel and express those emotions was extremely healing and cathartic. Before long, my tears of sadness and pain turned to tears of joy as I recognized just how much my friend cared about me and how much love I was feeling from her at that moment.

Me: *I am so glad we are having this conversation because I'm tired of pretending everything is okay. I have been hiding behind this new-age spiritual positive thinking mask for so long that I haven't allowed myself to feel my emotions. I guess a part of me believed that if I shared the negative things in my life, it meant that I didn't have faith that it would get better. But now I realize this isn't true. Just because I may be feeling sad or afraid does not mean that I've lost faith. It just means that I'm human and have feelings and should always be aware of and true to those feelings.*

Her: *The key to happiness is being in touch with how you truly feel and being able to express whatever you feel openly and honestly. Feelings are neither good nor bad; they just are. Emotions are just energy in motion, which is a human being's way of receiving internal feedback and then expressing their internal response to external stimuli. In reality, our emotions are the internal guidance system that keeps us in touch with our humanness.*

Now that we've had this conversation, I hope you will be able to speak with me openly and honestly about how you really feel, and you should know that negativity isn't necessarily bad.

Focusing on it too much can make matters worse, but the key is to always be honest with how you feel, no matter what situation you may be in. I accept you unconditionally as a friend and will be here for you even when things are tough. You don't have to impress me with your optimism and intellect because I accept you for who you are, not what you do. Do you understand?

Me: *I really do. This experience has been good for me and has opened my eyes to the fact that I still have some healing and some growing to do. Thank you so much for seeing through my positive mask and challenging me to take it off. I promise I will do my best to be as open and honest as possible when I'm speaking with you. Thank you so much for being my friend. I love you!*

After that conversation, I had to carry out some deep soul searching to figure out why it was so difficult to initially express my feelings to my friend. As I contemplated our conversation, I was able to see a pattern in my life that I had been using for a very long time. I always used positivity as a way of not expressing my true feelings to others, and I always sought other people's approval to feel good about myself.

I knew I wanted to break this pattern, and I decided to figure out what steps I needed to take to do so.

I decided to talk to my friend to see if she could begin shedding some light on my behavior. She informed me that one of the reasons why I may have had so much difficulty expressing my feelings could have been the result of some childhood trauma. She shared her experience of going to therapy to deal with some issues from her childhood, and she suggested that I consider therapy that may help me deal with my problems.

She then said something that stood out to me. It was a statement that was so powerful it literally caused me to rethink everything I had learned in the personal development arena. She looked at me and said, "I don't care how positive you are, how many books you read, or how many seminars you go to. Until you make peace with your past, you will never truly be happy."

This statement challenged me to examine my entire philosophy on personal development thoroughly.

I then realized that all the motivational seminars and books I had read did not help me make peace with my past, so I decided to make it the number one priority in my life. I intuitively knew that making peace with my past was the missing link to finding true happiness.

I recently ran across a quote by author and spiritual teacher Iyanla Vanzant that fully embodies why making peace with your past is so important. This powerful quote holds the key to your happiness and I suggest you read it slowly (several times) and intently so that you fully grasp the implications of its message.

> *"Until you heal the wounds of your past, you are going to bleed. You can bandage the bleeding with food, with alcohol, with drugs, with work, with cigarettes, with sex, but eventually, it will all ooze through and stain your life. You must find the strength to open the wounds, stick your hands inside, pull out the core of the pain that is holding you in your past, the memories, and make peace with them."*

Herein lies the key to your happiness. Over the last twenty years, I've learned that we must be willing to heal our hearts and make peace with our past if we truly want to be happy. We can read all the self-help books in the world and listen to audio programs or go to seminars with motivational speakers. Still, if we fail to carry out our healing work, we will unconsciously sabotage our lives and ultimately keep ourselves from being completely happy.

Amazingly, some people do not believe that their childhood can adversely affect their adult lives. Have you ever heard someone say that their parents used to beat them when they were little, yet they still turned out okay? This statement is a defense mechanism that keeps people trapped in their pain, and they will rationalize that their traumatic childhoods had no effect on them whatsoever. The truth is, if you remember being beaten as a child and have not done any healing work, I can assure you that it will affect your life today.

The key to making peace with your past lies in your willingness to heal any emotional scars you may carry from your childhood. Healing your heart is the key to making peace with your past. Psychologists will tell you that, at their core, all addictions have an unresolved emotional conflict, which simply means that emotional wounds need to be healed.

What Iyanla Vanzant meant when she said, *"You must find the strength to open the wounds, stick your hands inside, pull out the core of the pain that is holding you in your past, the memories, and make peace with them"* is that it is your responsibility to look within your own heart and find where the pain is and be willing to heal that pain.

There is a powerful scene in the movie Star Wars in which Luke Skywalker is being trained by the Master Teacher, Yoda. In the scene, Yoda tells Luke that he must enter a dark cave to face his demons and ultimately become a Jedi Knight. As Luke begins to look into the cave, he turns to Yoda and asks: "What's in the cave?" To which Yoda replies, "Only what you take with you." As Luke goes into the cave, he is confronted by his nemesis, Darth Vader. Darth Vader is the antagonist in the movie who embraces "The Dark Side." As Darth Vader approaches, Luke pulls out his Light Saber and begins fighting with him. After a brief battle, Luke chops off Darth Vader's head, and it appears he has defeated the bad guy. As Luke looks at the severed head, smoke suddenly comes from Vader's helmet. As the smoke clears, Luke looks inside the helmet and sees his own face.

The symbolism of this scene speaks directly to the importance of making peace with your past. Luke Skywalker represents the good in every human being, and his training with the Master represents the importance of teachers guiding us on our personal growth journeys to find the good within us. The dark cave represents the subconscious mind that stores your erroneous negative beliefs about yourself. It is the place where fear resides, and we must be willing to enter the cave if we truly want to make peace with our past and not live in fear.

Darth Vader represents the parts of ourselves that we are sometimes afraid to look at. He symbolizes our shadows, which are the parts of ourselves that we sometimes hide, suppress, or deny. The battle represents the struggle we must go through to shed light on the dark places in our minds and hearts that keep us from expressing who we really are. Cutting off Darth Vader's head and then Luke seeing his own face represents facing our demons within and allowing the dark parts of ourselves to die so that we can be resurrected into who we truly are.

The key is to remember what Yoda said about what's in the cave. "Only what you take with you." This means that the darkness we perceive is only in our minds. The so-called darkness is simply erroneous beliefs we hold about ourselves, and when we become courageous enough to face our inner darkness, that part of us dies, and the real part of us awakens.

Some people prescribe the idea that you do not have to address your childhood wounds in order to be successful and happy. They believe it does not do any good to "dig up" old hurts. I completely disagree with this way of thinking. I believe that it is absolutely imperative that you are willing to look at the dark events in your life and are willing to shed light on them. Those dark places will eventually sabotage your happiness if you are unwilling to do so.

There is a term called "spiritual bypassing," which means people refuse to heal their inner wounds because they have accepted a specific religious teaching that says God can heal them. I used to hold that belief. At one time, I thought that if I prayed enough and followed religious dogma and doctrine, I would eventually become happy. My own experience has taught me otherwise. It wasn't until I became courageous enough to make peace with my past and deal with some childhood trauma that I could heal my heart and become genuinely happy.

When I decided to heal my wounds, I was introduced to a man named John Bradshaw, who facilitated a program called Healing Your Inner Child. In one of his workshops, I learned how my abusive childhood was at the core of all the dysfunction in my life. I learned that I had abandonment issues due to being separated from my mom when I was six years old, and I also learned that for most of my adult life, I was driven by a deep sense of shame. It was my internal feelings of shame that drove me to be successful. I worked really hard to gain other people's approval because, deep down, I didn't feel worthy.

Although it was extremely difficult, I made a choice to heal my heart and make peace with my past. I took Iyanla's advice and found the strength to open my wounds, stick my hands inside, and pull out the core of my pain that was keeping me trapped in my past - and I made peace with them.

As a result of doing this work, I can honestly admit that I am happier today than I've ever been in my life. It definitely wasn't easy, but I can assure you that it was worth it.

I hope that you will take some time and really think about what I've just shared. Do not make the same mistakes I did in thinking that being positive will solve all your problems. Of course, there is absolutely nothing wrong with being positive, and I am still a huge advocate of positive thinking. The key is to ensure that you aren't hiding behind positivity because of some unresolved emotional pain like I did.

If you are committed to making peace with your past and are looking for ways to do so, let me make a few suggestions for you to consider. First of all, I think it's crucial that you are willing to seek support if needed. I realize that there is a lot of negative stigmas attached to seeking support, but that is a sign of strength, not weakness, when you seek help.

Here are a few things to consider if you are truly ready to make peace with your past.

1. Therapy

There is nothing wrong with seeking a good therapist to support you in dealing with any emotional challenges you may face. Our society has conditioned us to believe that we are supposed to carry the weight of the world on our shoulders and not seek support, but this simply isn't true. We all need support at one time or another, so if you've been looking for ways to help you make peace with your past, a good therapist may be exactly what you need.

I want to share an article I wrote a while ago that shares my first experience with therapy. I hope it will give you some insight into how difficult and challenging it might be and inspire you to take the first step if you think you will benefit from therapy. The article is titled "Men's Emotional Healing."

In 1989, I had a series of traumatic experiences that were beginning to take their toll. My divorce and separation from my kids were extremely painful and had begun to impact my life negatively. I had slipped into a deep state of depression and was barely able to function on a daily basis. As my depression deepened, I went into isolation, where I literally shut myself off from the outside world.

Although I could go to work and function in that capacity, I was completely disconnected from any social setting. I was not dating, and I did not socialize with my friends. I also had difficulty sleeping. I would rarely eat and had begun to lose weight, which was rare for me as a former personal trainer who took excellent care of my physical body. After several months, I began to have fleeting thoughts of suicide, and it appeared that my situation was hopeless. In an effort to alleviate some of the pain, I begin to read books dealing with depression.

As I read them, I could see myself in some of the stories. I definitely had all of the symptoms of depression, and I knew I had to deal with it head-on if I ever wanted to get my life back on track. After reading several books, I realized that I was still deeply depressed and had not begun to deal with the issues causing my depression. Instinctively, I knew I needed help, and I decided to seek therapy.

After deciding to get help, another series of challenges surfaced. First of all, how was I going to find a therapist? How would I know which one to choose? What if the therapist couldn't help me? Would I be able to change? Could therapy "fix" me? What about the money to pay for it? I was completely broke and definitely couldn't pay someone to listen to my problems. What was I going to do? These were just a few of the questions going through my mind.

My greatest fear was wondering what would happen if my employees found out. As a manager, I was considered the leader, and I definitely didn't want to appear weak in front of my co-workers. I believed that I needed to keep this a secret so I would not lose the respect of my employees. In addition, I did not want my superiors to know because I thought I might lose my job if they found out.

After a few months of agonizing over these questions, I knew I had to take the chance and try therapy. I didn't have any other choice. It was seek help or die - there was no gray area. I decided that I wanted to live and somehow gained the courage to seek a therapist.

My first attempt at therapy did not go well. I walked into the therapist's office and pretended to seek information for a friend. I'm sure the people there knew this was a lie, but they allowed me to walk out with some of their brochures and a phone number to their suicide hotline.

To be honest, I was absolutely terrified. But although I was scared, I knew I would have to gain the courage to try again. I waited a few days and tried a different therapist office. This time I had a completely different result.

As I walked into the office, I believe the receptionist picked up on my fear. I began asking her questions about depression and whether or not they had any books I could read. All of a sudden, a therapist walked out and began asking me questions. "May I help you?" she asked. "Not really; I'm just looking for a little information about depression." "Are you depressed?" "I'm not really sure," I answered. "Why don't you come inside and let's talk a little? Is that alright?" "I guess so."

As I followed her into her office, it felt as if my heart was going to jump out of my chest. I was so nervous and afraid that I was literally dripping with sweat. She obviously picked up on this and began to put my mind at ease.

"What is your name?"

"Michael"

"Well, Michael, I can sense that you are a little nervous, so let me start by asking what I can do to help you. Is there anything I can do for you?"

"Well, maybe. I have been doing some research about depression, and I think I'm depressed, but I'm really not sure."

"Do you feel depressed?"

"Based on what I've read so far, I think I am. But to be completely honest, I'm not sure I know exactly what depression is supposed to feel like. Does that make any sense to you?"

"It makes a lot of sense to me. Unfortunately, most men do not recognize how they feel. Men have been conditioned to disconnect from their emotions, making it extremely difficult to express how they really feel. Most men will tell you what they think, but they usually do not know how they feel. You apparently fit into this category."

"I'm not sure if I really understand what you're saying, but a part of me thinks that you're right."

You Must Make Peace With Your Past

"You just validated the point I made. You are currently speaking from an intellectual perspective instead of an emotional one. It sounds as if you are disconnected from your emotions."

"Let's assume that you're right. If I am disconnected from my emotions, how do I get reconnected? Do you have any books on how to do this?

"Unfortunately, you cannot reconnect to your emotions by reading books. For you to reconnect, you have to relearn how to feel. This can be accomplished through therapy with me or any trained therapist."

"I don't understand what you mean. But how long will it take if I decide to relearn how to feel?"

"I really can't answer that question. It's really up to you and your commitment to the work."

"What do you mean doing the work? What kind of work is involved?"

"In the therapeutic community, we use the word 'work' because it takes a considerable effort to heal yourself so that you can reconnect with your emotions. Doing the work means that you become willing to open yourself up on an emotional level. This can be quite difficult at times."

"Well, I believe I'm ready. I'm tired of being alone and want to experience some fun in my life again. I think I can do this, so how much will it cost?"

"I operate on a sliding scale based on your ability to pay. The most important thing is for you to make the commitment to yourself to heal, and we can address the money issue at a later date. Are you ready to begin? Let's set up a date and time to begin your healing."

"I just wanted to thank you for being so nice and understanding. The truth is I was about to run out of your office before you showed up. Now I am really glad that I came because I believe that you can help me."

"That is a great attitude to have. I'm glad that you trust me enough to work with you. Just remember that I can guide you, but you must be willing to do the work. As long as you believe that you can heal, I can assure you that you will. Just stay committed and trust the process, and you will be just fine. The truth is you have already done the hard part by showing up today. It takes incredible courage to be here, and I'm proud of you for taking the first step."

As I left the therapist's office that day, I knew I had just taken the biggest step of my life. I didn't know what to expect, but I knew I was willing to do whatever it took to heal my emotions and relearn how to feel. I became committed to my own healing, and I can now say that I'm emotionally healed and connected to my authentic self.

As the therapist mentioned, it wasn't easy, but it was definitely possible. It has been one of the most challenging yet most fulfilling journeys of my life.

I cannot put into words the joy I feel regularly as a result of carrying out my emotional work. My relationships now work, my creativity and sense of reverence are enhanced, my love of nature has been rekindled, and my professional life is rewarding and fulfilling. I took the road less traveled, and it has made all the difference in the world for me.

I wanted to share this story because there is such a negative stigma about men and therapy that I believe it's time for a new conversation. In this new conversation, men will recognize the importance of healing their emotions and put forth the effort to do their healing work.

When we learn to support each other in our growth, we can remove the fear and stigma of being emotionally vulnerable, which will ultimately make us happier. I personally believe that this is the most important work men can participate in, and we must begin supporting each other through this process.

If we gain the courage to do this work, we will see a decline in domestic violence, child abuse, alcoholism, fatherlessness, and random acts of violence. The time has come for a new conversation about our emotional healing.

Are you willing to join in the conversation?

So the first step in making peace with your past is to make sure that you do some emotional healing work. It may be in the form of therapy, but it could also be through support groups like AA.

2. Workshops/Seminars/Webinars

Several organizations offer inner-child healing workshops around the country. I suggest you research inner child work online and find a resource in your area. You will simply have to trust yourself and find one that feels right for you. You can begin by reading some books by John Bradshaw if you aren't comfortable attending the workshops. Two of my favorites are *Healing The Shame That Binds You* and *Homecoming*. I highly recommend that you pick up a copy of both.

The key is to become 100% committed to healing your heart and making peace with your past. Once you commit and then take action, rest assured you will begin to feel better about your life, and it will definitely get easier. It may not be an easy process, but I promise you it will be well worth it.

Personal development seminars are also powerful ways to make peace with your past. If you have never done anything like this before, you're simply going to have to trust me. There are countless seminars available that can support you in making peace with your past. There are one-day seminars, three-day retreats, online webinars, and a wide variety of others that can assist you along your journey. Here are just a few that I have found extremely helpful.

You Must Make Peace With Your Past

I highly recommend a three-day workshop called The New Warrior Training Adventure if you are male. It is carried out by an organization called The Mankind Project, and without question, it is one of the most transformational experiences you will ever encounter.

You can find out more about them at: www.mkp.org.

If you are female, they have a sister organization called The Woman Within, which offers similar training for women, and I'm sure it will be transformational as well.

You can find them at: www.womanwithin.org.

Another seminar I highly recommend is called the Landmark Forum. (www.landmarkworldwide.com) It is a powerful transformational experience that provides you with the tools to create the life you know you deserve. I like to think of the program as a wake-up call to life, and I can assure you that it will provide the spark to help you ignite your inner passions and purpose.

The key is to become 100% committed to making peace with your past. You have to want it more than anything. You have to listen to that still, small voice within you that is calling you to do this work. It's all up to you!

I am absolutely convinced that making peace with your past is a surefire way to achieve true freedom and happiness. As I've mentioned, it won't be easy, but it will definitely be worth it. If you commit to doing this, I can promise you that you will experience deep inner peace, less anxiety, no more depression, a deeper sense of passion and purpose, and a deep inner knowing that you can create the life of your dreams.

Isn't that what you want - a more rewarding and fulfilling life experience? If the answer is yes, begin by making peace with your past, and I can assure you that you will have everything you need to do so.

I would like to close this chapter with a quote from the Dalai Lama. He was once asked what he found most fascinating about human beings, and this is the answer he gave:

"Man sacrifices his health in order to make money. Then he sacrifices money to recuperate his health. And then he is so anxious about the future that he does not enjoy the present moment. As a result, he does not live in the present or the future, he lives as if he is never going to die, and then he dies having never truly lived."

Make sure you do not make this mistake. Making peace with your past will give you many reasons to make sure that your life is well lived and that you have no regrets. Do not die with your music still in you. Learn to sing your song so that the whole world hears you, and you will experience the joy that defies human understanding.

Live your life out loud! You can do this!

"Let's make sure every class has the same opportunity going forward because we are enough to take care of our own community. We are enough to ensure we have all of the opportunities of the American dream, and we will show it to each other through our actions and through our words and through our deeds."
- Robert Smith

Chapter 6

You Must Create A Positive Support Network

by

Jermaine Johnson

I remember my first day of middle school. Entering the 6th grade, I was full of childhood fears and anxiety. This was a new school in a new district where hundreds of kids were arriving at this building that appeared to be the size of a thousand football fields. I didn't know anyone in this crowd of strangers, and my emotions were so strong that I could feel them vibrating in my body. Trying to complete the simple tasks I had during the day, like finding my next class, locating the gym, and which period was lunch time seemed extremely daunting.

Toward the middle of the day, as I cautiously walked through the hallway to my next class, waiting on some giant super senior to demand my lunch money, I heard a voice in the distance that was very familiar to me. My eyes wide open and my heart beating out of my chest with excitement, I got closer and saw what I thought at the time was "The greatest thing that ever happened to me." Jude Pierre!

I met Jude in Kindergarten years earlier. He was, and is, my oldest friend. We had every class together from kindergarten to 5th grade. Leaving P.S. 36 elementary school and going to a different district for middle school at I.S. 74, I was so surprised to see a familiar face. To top it off, Jude also lived close to my neighborhood, so I would have a friend to ride with on the two buses it took to get to this new school. This was a game-changer!

Jude was also very glad to see me. A familiar face. He would later tell me about the fear and anxiety that he was experiencing that day and how relieved he was to see me. I was shocked to learn that he was experiencing the same thing because all the other kids seemed to be completely comfortable in this new environment. Maybe they thought we were too.

We would meet new people during the first week and bring them into our small group. David came first, then Greg came after. All of the anxiety and fear from that first week dissipated, and I was beginning to feel right at home. This was the first time I ever experienced how important it was to have a support network.

The crew and I stuck close together through our middle school years. Jude and Greg were star basketball players, while David and I focused on making music and writing songs. We went to every basketball game and cheered on the star players, while Jude and Greg would be the first ears to listen to our songs even before they were finished.

We would get together at lunch and after school to rap all the lyrics to the songs we created that day. They became our feedback loop for what lyrics moved them and which ones were not so great. We were each doing what we loved and leaned on each other for feedback, criticism, direction, and the "Even Better Ifs."

A few years later, I found myself in the auditorium on stage, receiving my diploma with my three best buddies who had supported me for the last three years. This was a very exciting time for us. The crowd was full with our friends and family cheering and yelling our names after we were called to shake hands with the school principal and receive that piece of paper we all worked so hard to get. Smiling from ear to ear as I exited the stage in my signature cool-ass dance moves, the crowd responded in laughter just as I planned it. I felt like The Man!

Soon, the feeling of jubilee and excitement began to subside as the conversation shifted to a discussion about what was next—high School. The thing is, we were not all going to the same school, and the reality of not being together was beginning to hit home in a big way. Each of us was "Man" now, so we're all pretending in front of each other like "We got this," knowing that we were all scared shitless! For the first time in our relationship, I was uncomfortable telling my best friends that I was really scared and sad that we would not be together in High School. I wanted them to believe that I was tough and confident and would survive and thrive whether they were with me or not. The truth was, I was screaming inside, "PLEASE DON'T LEAVE ME." I held that energy until later that night when I cried myself to sleep in private. This was the first time I remember successfully creating a "Mask" to hide my true feelings. I will go on to wear this mask in public for the next thirty years.

At age 27, I got married. At age 32, I started a successful business that I operate to this day. By age 35, I became aware that I was living two lives and, at times, multiple lives. At the time, my belief was simply that "Everyone has multiple lives," and I was no different. I can't possibly be the same person in front of my parents that I am with my friends. I can't act like "Me" when I'm around my children. They would be petrified! I can't possibly be the version of me that my homeboys know while I'm out with my wife. So it only makes sense that I create multiple personalities so I can be accepted in whatever circle I am in at the time. Later on, I would begin to identify these different iterations of myself as my "Masks."

By age 40, I was married, healthy, successful, and very busy. It's everything I thought I always wanted. I have achieved the American dream. My wife and I had brand new high-end cars, my children were in school and learning the company business, and my oldest daughter became a mother and made me a proud grandfather. WOW! Life was great! Or so it seemed to the outside world. These versions of me that I created have taken over and it has become increasingly more difficult for me to find the authentic me. The true me.

What I felt inside was not what I was projecting on the outside. I felt trapped inside my own body and didn't know how to correct the course. I realized then that I have not been the authentic me since I was twelve years old.

Thankfully, I learned somewhere in passing to occasionally take self-inventory. Maybe it was from one of the many self-help books I read by some guru of life; who knows? One of the first things that came up for me was, where are my real friends? Where are those boys who supported me through middle school? Why do my current friends not show up on my radar when I ask the question? I have so many "Friends" around me right now, so why do I feel so alone? Why can't I tell these men the truth about what I'm experiencing? Why am I suffering in silence when I seem to have an army of people around me who call themselves my friends? These questions haunted me for the next three years as I began to pay attention to my surroundings, trying to answer these questions. I came up with nothing.

At 45, tired of trying to self-assess and still feeling empty, I decided to do the one thing I thought I would never do - to speak to a therapist. At first, I felt like a failure. I believed that only weak people needed therapy. After all, I was a Man's Man and the leader of every group in my life. Everyone looked to me for all the answers because I was the one who had it all, and had it all together. They only knew the mask I presented to them, so I understand why they felt that way. I crafted my masks with incredible accuracy, so they were very effective at hiding those parts of me that I judged to be weak.

For the sake of this chapter, I will refer to this therapist as Bee. She would later be the genesis of what I now refer to as entering my "Mature Adult" life. We initially met twice per week, and for the first few weeks, I employed ALL the masks I could muster up. I even tried to design some on the fly when I began feeling too vulnerable by the incredibly accurate probing questions Bee would ask. Thankfully, she was just as good at spotting these different personalities as I was at making them up. It was an epic battle that Bee was fully prepared for and ready to go the distance with this veteran of repressing feelings.

The Brothahood of Kings

During one of my sessions a few months in, Bee asked me a question that eventually led us down the conversational road of the impacts of slavery intergenerationally. As we explored this area of my memory, history, and family lineage, we began to unpack some of the possible origins of the choices I made in my life. Bee is a very visual and bioenergetic teacher, so she would always pull out visual aids or have us get up and do something physical to incorporate the learnings of the day and anchor the feelings that may come up for me. At the end of our session, she offered me a book to read that she thought may help me understand more about the male psyche and the rituals of male initiations that were lost during the middle passage.

As I began to read the book, I found myself glued to the pages. It's like this book was talking to me on a level that I didn't even know existed. It was powerful to me, but not like I was used to. It was as if my spirit was connecting to some higher intelligence that was not of this world. The book had words on the page, just like any other book I had read in the past, but now I could feel the messages behind the words, and it took on a life of its own. At the time, I was traveling from Atlanta to Miami regularly, so I ordered the audiobook so I could really dive deeper into this new learning. I read the book twice and listened to the audiobook four times. This book has essentially helped me change the way I process my life, my choices, and the reasons behind those choices.

You Must Create A Positive Support Network

One thing that the book revealed was my need for authentic connection with other men. I started on a quest to find a group of men I could fellowship with, get support, give support, and hopefully learn more about how to become a better version of myself. I realized that the way I found support as a child is not the same way I should find support as an adult. It has to be intentional, focused, and very specific to meet the needs I'm facing today in a mature way.

On my google search, many groups came up on the list, but only one stood out to me—The Mankind Project (MKP). I clicked on the website, and as I read the landing page, I had to pinch myself to see if I was dreaming. This group's description was as if the author of this book started a support group using the framework and basic principles that the book set forth. This felt again like the book was speaking to me directly. I knew at that moment that this was where I was supposed to be.

I called the number on the website and spoke to a representative that honored me for taking the first step in creating the life I chose to live. How could he know that!?! I was stunned by how it seemed as if they were waiting for me to call. This further reinforced my belief that I was exactly where I belonged. The representative answered all my questions and invited me to attend a weekend gathering of men scheduled to occur in three weeks. He gave me all the info I needed. I registered and waited with anticipation for this weekend to come. I packed my overnight bag and some recommended essentials and embarked on the journey I'd been waiting for all my life.

To become initiated as a New Warrior and begin my journey into conscious, mature masculinity. When I arrived at the campsite, I entered this training as a man's man. Confident, successful, angry, full of myself, and ready for anything. When I emerged from that weekend three days later, I was entirely different.

The NWTA (New Warrior Training Adventure). The signature training of The Mankind Project.

On this weekend, Men held space for me to see those parts of me that I repressed throughout my life. In essence, I forgot that these parts of me even existed. These men asked me powerful questions that continued to invite me to go deeper and deeper into those places I had been hiding for years. They held me while I revisited those events in my life that helped shape me over the many years and taught me that as a mature man (New Warrior), I have the power to make a different choice today if I choose to. These were very powerful lessons for me because I was unaware at that time that this was the origin of all my suffering. This new awareness excited me to want to know more about men's work, so I jumped in with both feet. I connected with men who have been in MKP for many years and began my own journey of learning and

You Must Create A Positive Support Network

mastering this new technology that looked like magic to me when I watched these processes transform men's lives right in front of my eyes. It was the give-and-take that I was most attracted to. Both holding space for men to do their work and learning something new about myself in the process. The deeper I got, the more I understood myself on a deeper level, yet something was still missing in my experience. It took me a year or two to figure out what the deficit was that I felt in my body while learning and practicing this new way of being. I needed to do this work with other men who looked like me. Men who have experienced this world in the way that I did. Men who understood what it was like to come of age as a historically not included individual. I needed Black Men.

Unfortunately, in MKP, not many black men participated in Men's work. We were scattered all over the world, so most of us didn't know the rest of us even existed within the organization. I expressed my need to one of my mentors in my local area.

This mentor is a white man with who I have grown close. I learned a great deal about Men's work through his willingness to take me under his wing and share his journey. He connected me with a man out of Texas who he thought may be a great resource for me in connecting with other Black Men who are doing the work. The introductory email went out, and I got a reply two days later. "Welcome Brother. I would love to connect by phone with you this week when you have time. In the meanwhile, I will add you to our email list group. Our group name is AFAM (African American Warriors of MKP)." I was both shocked and excited! It seems other Black men wanted the same thing as me. There is a group within MKP dedicated to Black Men doing their work. As I read the final pieces of the email and got down to the signature line, it read, "Judge Mattocks Jr."

This man would go on to be the Mentor I needed, the friend I was looking for, and the teacher that would elevate my skill level and support me in nurturing my leadership skills. Two weeks later, I sat in my first virtual Group Circle with all Black Men from different parts of the country. This group was the most powerful, uplifting, and joyful experience that I have had since middle school. I attended every group every week for the next year. Doing my work with Men who look like me took me to places I could've never anticipated. I was finally becoming the Man I truly wanted to be.

Over the next few years, I realized that we needed more than just a weekly group and an email list. We needed to organize in a way that invited Black Men to do their work, bring new Men into the work, and become the leaders our communities desperately need. In close consultation with Judge Mattocks and the men in our group, we decided to create the experience we wanted to see within MKP. We wanted Black Men to know that this was a safe space where they could be supported, give support, learn new skills, sharpen existing skills, and tackle the issues we share as people of color. We wanted to assemble in a way that keeps us in constant contact with each other and highly visible to new Black Men coming into the work so they know we are here. This was especially important for me because I was that man who felt alone, not knowing where the other Men of Color were within the organization. We set out to accomplish this goal. It began with the inception of "The Brothahood of MKP."

The Brothahood of MKP is a community within a community that is focused on the coordination and empowerment of all Black, Indigenous, and Men of Color within MKP. We create training, Groups, Intensive weekends, and gatherings of men focused on us and our experience. It is a space created by us to do our work and learn with each other. The intention is to empower black men to be the leaders we need in their local communities where they might be the only person of color sitting in groups and doing their work. We come together to decompress, share the burdens of being black in the USA, and process that experience in a good way. I hope this empowers us to go back into the world strong and confident to lead the charge in creating Diversity, Equity, and Inclusion in our world.

The evolution of The Brothahood of MKP is The Brothahood of Kings Collective. Here, we collaborate and co-create the initiatives that directly impact our communities. The talented men in The Brothahood of Kings create content, facilitate groups, create outreach platforms on social media, build websites to service our communities, partner up with other organizations doing great things for people of color, and provide opportunities for Black Men to step into leadership roles that help them meet the needs of their communities while keeping an emphasis on personal growth, self-care, and self-awareness. In essence, it is the support system I always wanted and needed to feel whole as a Man among Men embarking on my Hero's Journey.

It is paramount to have a support network to consciously embark on a Hero's Journey or to intentionally set out to create the best version of you. It is also important to create that network in the way that works best for you. Every Man's journey is his own, so how it is crafted is very personal. There is no "one-size-fits-all" approach because we are all one of a kind. A one-of-one. There is only one me. I alone have the blueprint designs of how "I" desire to show up in the world.

We are not aware at the time, but every day of our lives, we practice behaviors that we learn from others, whether intended or unintended. We are mimicking learned behaviors from our experiences and practicing them daily to ensure we don't forget them. Almost 100% of this is happening subconsciously. Most of what we do today are learned behaviors from parents, uncles, aunties, pastors, teachers, counselors, friends, TV shows, movies, social media, and all other forms of social communication. It's not inherently bad until it begins to impact our lives negatively.

You Must Create A Positive Support Network

The real work happens when we become aware of these practices, take a deeper dive into where we picked up the behaviors, honor that space, and choose to make a different choice. Once we make the new choice, we have to begin a new conscious practice to help us reinforce and anchor it in our daily lives, similar to how we practiced and reinforced the unconscious behaviors that we didn't choose. Here is where your support system becomes vital.

Since this new practice is intentional, it is important that your support network is intentional and includes men who are also on a similar journey. When you want to work out and build muscles, surround yourself with bodybuilders. The same principle applies here. Changing habits, behaviors, and certain choices can often be challenging, especially when you've been living the old habits, behaviors, and choices for many years. As you intentionally practice your new way of being, you may often experience yourself reverting to your old way of being. It is here that you can lean into your support network and process what happened, what triggered you, what you can do moving forward, and what new tools may be at your disposal to deal with whatever feelings and judgments may come up for you. It is also in this space where men can offer you support and point out things you may have missed.

Life has a way of testing our ability to stay on course. Our job is to meet that resistance and endure. When our support network is strong, and we surround ourselves with intentional allies who are willing to offer support and accountability, hold space for us to journey into those parts of ourselves that we may hide, repress, or deny, and show us love when we feel like no one else does. We give ourselves the gift of creating an extraordinary life by having the courage to change what is not serving us.

"Everyone that you meet comes with baggage. Find someone who loves you enough to help you unpack."
– Unknown.

Chapter 7

Prioritize Relationships

I'd like you to take a moment and think about the current state of your relationships. On a scale of 1-10, I'd like you to rate your relationships. I'm aware there are different types of relationships, so for this exercise, I'd like you to focus on relationships with a significant other—wife, girlfriend, spouse, baby mama, etc. If you have a loving relationship, give yourself a 10. Your score will be much lower if your relationship is filled with drama and fighting.

Be completely honest with yourself; what's your score?

The purpose of the exercise isn't to judge you for your relationships. The intention is for you to decide if you like the current status of your relationships. If you didn't score a 10, would you like to?

I'm sure some of you reading this may not believe it's possible to score a 10, but rest assured, it is possible. The reason I say

Prioritize Relationships

this is because, currently, I would rate my marriage as a 10. I have been happily married for almost 21 years now, and I can honestly say that I absolutely love being married.

Like most men, my relationships haven't always been a 10. I've been divorced, had several failed relationships, and was even engaged once and then ended the relationship three weeks before the wedding. I definitely know the pain and heartache of failed relationships, but I also know the joy of finding the right person to share your life with.

I want to share some lessons I've learned as a happily married man and a certified life coach. I am convinced that any man can create great relationships, but he has to be willing to learn how to do so.

The first lesson I'd like to share is how being stuck on the societal rollercoaster can keep you from creating great relationships.

When I got married the first time, I got married for all the wrong reasons. I was twenty-one years old and was climbing the corporate ladder. I thought being married would help me appear more mature and advance my career. By the age of twenty-two, I had become a manager for a multi-million dollar building supply company, which at the time, was the youngest manager in the history of the company. I was also only the second black manager in its fifty-six-year history.

The Brothahood of Kings

When I was twenty-three, I purchased my first home and was living the American Dream. From the outside, I looked as if I had it all together. But something was wrong that I really couldn't put my finger on.

After a few years, my wife and I began having problems. We would argue a lot, so I would stay at work most of the time to avoid her. She would then get upset because I was working so much, which caused us to move further apart.

In my mind, I was right and she was wrong. I justified working so much by saying I was working hard for her and my family so we could have a good life. The truth was, I was stuck on the rollercoaster doing everything society said I was supposed to do, and I honestly didn't know what I was doing wrong.

One night we were having an argument and I mentioned she didn't appreciate how hard I was working. I told her to look around at the nice house I had bought her and the nice car she was driving. She then looked at me and said something that I'll never forget. She said, "This is a nice house, and I appreciate you buying it for me. But the truth is, I would have been just as happy in our apartment as long as I was with you."

In retrospect, I realize that she meant every word she said. But at the time, I took it the wrong way and got extremely angry at her. Her words validated my belief that she didn't appreciate my hard work, and I attacked her for being unappreciative.

Prioritize Relationships

After that fight, our marriage spiraled downward, and eventually, we ended up getting a divorce. Of course, there were lots of other problems in our marriage, but for me, feeling unappreciated was the straw that broke the camel's back.

After some deep self-introspection and lots of emotional healing, I learned to take responsibility for my part in the divorce. I learned that one of the reasons I couldn't accept that my wife really loved me was because of my emotional baggage from an abusive childhood. I had to be willing to let go of that baggage in order to understand I was wrong for arguing with her about not appreciating me for buying the house. She did love me and wanted nothing more than just to be with me.

I learned from my first marriage that I was on a societal rollercoaster and had no idea how to make a marriage work. I was in complete denial of my emotional baggage, which was the real reason my marriage failed.

I want to share a conversation that completely changed my view of relationships and allowed me to actually figure out why my relationships had been so difficult. I was having a pity party with a very good female friend, and I was venting my frustrations to her.

The conversation went something like this.

The Brothahood of Kings

Me: "You women are always talking about how difficult it is to find a good man, but why do you women always leave good men once you find them?"

Her: "What do you mean, Michael?"

Me: "Well, the last few women I've dated have all said the same thing when they broke up with me. Each of them has said they care too much about me to stay in the relationship. That makes no sense to me. How can you care about someone and leave them at the same time? I can't understand that?"

Her: "Is that all they said?"

Me: "They also said I was emotionally unavailable, but I disagree with that. I'm a nice guy and easy to get along with. I don't understand what they mean when they say I'm emotionally unavailable."

Her: "Well, Michael, you are my good friend, and I care a lot about you. Are you open to a truth bomb that just may help you figure out why your relationships aren't working?"

Me: "Absolutely! Drop that truth bomb on me right now! I'm ready to hear it!"

Her: "Alright, here it goes, be sure to let it soak in before you respond. Here it is: If one person calls you a jackass, you probably shouldn't worry about it, but if two or more do, then you might want to get a saddle. Have you not noticed that you are the only common denominator in all of your relationships? Maybe the problem isn't the women in your life; perhaps the problem is you."

Initially, I sat there in shock. At first, I was going to get defensive and defend my point of view. But I trusted my friend's judgment and knew deep down inside that what she said was true.

As I sat there and thought about what she said, I had a light bulb moment. I realized that if I ever wanted to create a great relationship, I would have to be willing to examine why I was emotionally unavailable in relationships. Instead of blaming the women in my life, I needed to take 100% responsibility for my actions and figure out how to become emotionally available in my relationships.

This conversation completely changed my life and my view of relationships. At that moment, I made a conscious decision that I would take full responsibility for my relationships and stop blaming women. This decision changed my life and was the beginning of my emotional healing journey.

As a result of going on my emotional journey, I was able to heal my childhood trauma and unpack my emotional baggage. After doing so, I was able to create truly authentic relationships, which eventually led me to find the relationship of my dreams, which is how I was able to create a 10 in my marriage.

So, what is the key to creating great relationships and having deep connections with others? Creating a great relationship with yourself. This means you are willing to identify any unhealed or past traumas from your childhood or adulthood. The adage is true, "You can never truly love another until you learn to love yourself." So, self-love is the key to creating great relationships.

I want to share a story of one of my relationships that ended because of me being emotionally unavailable. Rest assured there is a very powerful message in the story if you're willing to look at it.

I met a woman at the gym who was absolutely gorgeous. On a scale of 1-10, she was honestly a 12. She had a near-perfect body, had a great job, drove a nice car, and was extremely fun to be with. After a couple of dates, I asked her if she would like to go to a pool party one of my neighbors was having. She agreed, and on the day of the party, she showed up in a two-piece bikini and was absolutely stunning.

We walked down the street to my neighbor's house, and when we walked in, all of my friends' jaws literally dropped. Of course, I was filled with pride as my friends all stared at how beautiful she was, and of course, my ego received a big

Prioritize Relationships

boost. We had a wonderful time at the party, and afterward, we returned to my place and had a few drinks and a few laughs. She told me she was happy that my friends found her so attractive, and she specifically wore the bikini to impress my friends. I thanked her for making me look so good and appreciated her allowing me to show her off to my friends.

A few days later, I was hanging out with my friends, and of course, the topic of conversation was my date. They all wanted to know where and how we met, and the single guys wanted to know the secret to finding such a beautiful woman.

Interestingly enough, no one ever asked what type of woman she was. The only thing they were concerned with was her external physical beauty, and of course, so was I. What I realize in retrospect is I was definitely proud to have my friends admire me for having been with such a beautiful woman, but deep down inside, I really felt insecure about my ability to create a deep relationship that would allow me to keep her.

Internally, I had a deep fear of abandonment, which would ultimately sabotage my relationships. My fear of abandonment caused me to try to do everything right to keep her in a relationship with me. I was extremely nice and supportive, attentive to her needs, and able to satisfy her sexually. On the surface, it appeared I was doing everything right. But unfortunately, my relationship pattern showed up again, so I was obviously doing everything wrong.

The Brothahood of Kings

One night while lying in bed, she asked me to share how I really felt about her. She also asked why I never mentioned if I missed her when she was away. As I thought about it, I knew I wasn't in love with her, but I also knew I cared deeply about her. But I honestly didn't know what to say. I enjoyed being with her but honestly didn't know how to share how I felt about her. She then commented on my inability to express how I felt and said she was afraid of getting emotionally close to me because she knew I was emotionally unavailable.

I then became angry because I thought I was doing everything right in the relationship, and now she was saying I wasn't emotionally available. I tried to explain to her that my actions should have told her how much I cared about her, but her reply was my actions couldn't express how I felt about her; only the words from my heart could relay the feelings I had for her. Since I couldn't verbalize how I felt, she didn't believe I really cared about her.

After that conversation, our relationship changed, and eventually, she left, saying she cared too much about me to stay in the relationship. When we broke up, she was crying and saying that she had so much love to give to me, but she knew I was incapable of reciprocating that love back to her, and she wasn't willing to give so much and not receive it back from me. She said that was her reason for leaving, and at the time, I truly didn't understand her reasoning, but because of my growth, I now know exactly what she meant and why she left.

Prioritize Relationships

Although I was sad when she left, a part of me was in complete denial. I rationalized it in my head by saying she didn't know what she was missing. I'm a good man and I know there are lots of fish in the sea, so I'll just have to find the one that is right for me. I denied my sadness and never admitted that I didn't want to break up with her. She was an amazing woman, but I simply didn't have the emotional tools to create intimacy and connection with her at the time, so I rationalized it by saying it was her loss, not mine. Deep down inside, though, I really wished she hadn't left. If I'm completely honest with myself, I actually did love her, but I didn't know how to express it.

Can you see the pattern in my relationships? Women actually cared about me and wanted to be with me, but because of my emotional unavailability, they would leave. I believe this is the greatest challenge we have as men regarding relationships. We do not know how to be emotionally available.

But why? Why do we struggle with emotional availability?

Do you remember the five illusions of manhood I spoke about in the previous chapter? Illusion number one is, "to be a man, you must be non-emotional and disconnected." This is the reason we struggle with being emotionally available. When we are trapped in this illusion, we disconnect from our emotions and cannot express how we really feel. Our feelings are the language of our soul, and without our feelings, we cannot connect emotionally.

For us to be relational, we must be willing to be emotional, which is extremely difficult, if not impossible, if you are trapped in this illusion.

After reading this, you may wonder if it's worth it and if it is possible to create a rewarding and fulfilling relationship. I say the answer is an emphatic YES! As a matter of fact, I will go as far as to say, relationships are the glue that holds our lives together; without them, our lives are really incomplete.

As I've mentioned, I honestly love being married and I make my marriage a very high priority in my life. My marriage comes before my business, friends, children, and even mom. My wife is the first priority after my relationship with my Creator and myself.

So rest assured, it is definitely possible for you to create the relationship of your dreams, but you're going to have to be willing to put forth the effort to do so.

If you're truly ready to do so, I'd like to share ten keys to creating healthy relationships. Rest assured, if you follow these keys, you can create the relationship of your dreams.

Number 1:

Develop a healthy relationship with yourself. For most men, I can assure you, it is very uncomfortable for them to say, "I love myself." Why? Because for some people, that may sound a little arrogant, a little cocky, a little narcissistic. The truth is, if you don't love yourself, you cannot love another person. It's not possible because all relationships begin with you. The first thing you have to be willing to do is create a healthy relationship with yourself. When you look in the mirror, ask yourself what do you see? Do you see someone that's trustworthy? Do you see someone that's lovable? Do you see someone that's dependable? Do you see someone in that mirror with whom you would want to be in a relationship? Ask yourself that question honestly because that's where relationships begin.

They begin with you. If you want to create healthy relationships, start with yourself. Sometimes that means we have to take a break from relationships with others and spend some time developing a relationship with ourselves. This may be uncomfortable or seem a little weird, but rest assured, it is the first thing you must do. Too often, we want to point our fingers at the women in our lives, but the fact remains that if we want to create healthy relationships, it always begins with the man in the mirror. We must take complete responsibility for our relationships and not blame anyone else except ourselves. Once we do this, we lay the foundation for great relationships.

Number 2:

Make relationships a top priority. In our culture and society, a man's job has been three things: procreate, protect, and provide. This has been true since the beginning of time. Think about it. What was a caveman's primary responsibility? He was supposed to find a cave to keep his little cavewoman happy and warm, and then he had to go out there to find food and ensure that he kept the dinosaurs from eating his family. Provide and protect.

Unfortunately, too many men are still trying to do that. They believe that if they just do these three things, then they will be happy. What we really need to do if we're going to make relationships a top priority is to connect; not just provide and protect, but connect. Connection takes emotions, and too many times, men do not have the emotional awareness to connect, which is a major cause of relationship failure.

We usually focus all of our attention on our jobs, bills, cars, staff, and kids, but we aren't doing anything to connect in our relationships. We aren't doing anything to deepen our connection.

Prioritize Relationships

The sad part is that many men will go through life and work at a career, raise their kids, and do everything they can to try and keep up with the Joneses. Then they get close to retirement and start asking themselves, "What am I going to do?"

As soon as they retire and they're at home with their wives full-time, it's total chaos because now they have to connect with their spouses, but they don't know how to do that.

If they had made relationships a top priority in their lives from the beginning, it would have made their lives a lot easier in the long run. Be sure to make relationships a top priority in your life, and you, too, will be happier in the long run.

Number 3:

Relinquish the need to be right. That's it! Let go of the need to be right! It's sad, but most men would rather be right than happy. They get attached to being right, which creates disconnection, and then they wonder why they're so unhappy.

Did you know that in healthy, connected relationships, two people never have to fight? What do you mean, Michael? A relationship without fighting? That's not possible! Yes, it is! I can promise you that it is possible, and here's how: you must distinguish between fighting and conflict. They aren't the same thing. Fighting is about being right. It's about being more concerned with being right than being happy.

On the other hand, conflict is what occurs when you bring two human beings together who will always have different opinions and beliefs. There's no way you can avoid conflict in a relationship, but you can let go of your need to be right about the conflict, which will instantly transform your relationships.

How many times have you fought over something really simple, and all you had to do was say, "That's okay," and let it go? But then there was a part of you that took this firm stand that you would just not let her be right. We've all done it. It's part of human nature to want to be right. Guess what? It doesn't work in relationships. Relinquishing your need to be right will transform your relationships in an instant if you will just be willing to let things go.

At the same time, there will be some things that you feel very strongly about, and you will choose not to compromise. You can do that without being attached to being right. You don't have to compromise your values in what's really important to you; you just have to be willing to say, "I don't have to be right. I'd rather be happy than right." When you do that, your relationships will transform immediately.

Number 4:

Be attentive to your partner. Being attentive to your partner means being in the present moment, fully aware of what they're saying, doing, and feeling. When we do that, we create a connection. When you pay attention to your partner and are concerned about what they're saying, connection is created. To create healthy relationships, you must be attentive to your partner; again, it creates a connection.

Number 5:

Express affection to your partner. That doesn't mean you have to go out in the street and kiss your wife in front of many people. Affection means that you're in some way affirming that you care about her by touching, acknowledging, and possibly kissing her. Affection doesn't necessarily mean kissing; you can just touch someone and show affection. The key is to be comfortable making physical contact with your partner. Touching is a way to create a physical connection. Studies have shown that infants that are held and nurtured and physically touched are healthier than babies that aren't. It's in our DNA to be touched and held. Expressing affection shouldn't be a big issue unless you're stuck in your male ego, so let that go. Express affection to your partner.

Number 6:

Say I love you and mean it. If you truly love someone, why should it be difficult to tell them? When you say, "I love you," be sure to say it from your heart, not your head. Say it often, and mean it every time. If you don't feel it, don't say it.

Number 7:

Spend quality time with your partner. You have to define quality time, but quality time means you move away from all the hustle and bustle of life, the kids, the jobs, the house, and all of that, and you spend time where you're just hanging out. For some, it may mean just sitting on the back porch. For others, it may be going to a spa all day. You have to decide what it is, but you must spend quality time where you're being attentive, and where you're connecting with your partner. It's extremely, extremely important.

Number 8:

Loosen up, let go, and have some fun. When was the last time you laughed with your partner? Just had a good laugh? If nothing comes to mind, something's wrong because relationships should be about fun, not just stress and all the day-to-day challenges we deal with. If you want to create a connection, you have to have fun because whether we realize it or not, we all have this playfulness inside us. It's there. Too many of us have pushed it down so far we've forgotten what it feels like, but we have to bring that playfulness back up and have fun and recognize that it doesn't make you less of a man to do so.

Number 9:

Celebrate your victories together. Life is tough enough as it is. Just look around you. We have all these things going on in the world. Our one refuge should be our relationship and our homes. When you accomplish something or something positive happens in your relationship, you should celebrate that. It can be something as small as a hug or as elaborate as taking your wife out to a fine dinner because she got a promotion at work. The key is to recognize that you're in this together, and you should be grateful that you have each other. When you overcome hurdles, that deepens your connection. Have some fun, celebrate your victories together, and acknowledge each other for being there for one another.

Number 10:

Count your blessings, not your problems. Too often, we focus all our attention on what's wrong versus what's right with our relationships. When you focus all your attention on what's wrong, guess what happens? Disconnection. If you're in a relationship, it may not be perfect, but you know this person is there for you, and that's something to be grateful for. Count your blessings for what she does right. An attitude of gratitude goes a long, long way in deepening your connection in relationships. Make sure that you're counting your blessings, not your problems. I can assure you that connection happens and relationships bloom when you do that. That's just the way that it works.

There they are, The 10 Keys To Creating Healthy Relationships. As men, we must put more emphasis on our relationships. We must make them a top priority. Unfortunately, very few men are willing to put forth the effort in doing the emotional healing work that makes great relationships possible, but since you're reading this book, you are definitely not like most men.

Unfortunately, sometimes relationships and marriages will come to an end, so I wanted to close this chapter by sharing an article I wrote titled Bouncing Back From Divorce. It summarizes what I've been saying so far in this chapter and I'm sure it will provide some insights that can support you if you're dealing with divorce or a breakup and want to eventually create great relationships.

"I WANT A DIVORCE!" Although it's been over thirty years since I heard these words, I still remember the shock and uncertainty I felt when my former wife screamed them at me. Although I knew there were problems in our marriage, I really didn't believe that they were insurmountable. I knew that I was unhappy and felt trapped in a situation that I could not get out of, but now that I had a way out, I was unprepared to deal with it. I remember sitting up late that night and pondering my next step. Should I go along with it and end our six-year marriage? What about the kids? Should I fight for custody? What will my friends and co-workers think? Where will I live? Should I give up the house? These were just a few questions running through my mind, and I had no idea how I would answer them.

The first few days after her divorce requests were terrible. We would not speak to each other or even make direct eye contact. Although we continued to sleep in the same bed, we were emotionally miles apart. We would simply go through our routines and walk past each other without saying a word. I could feel the tension between us, but I felt powerless to do anything. Whenever I attempted to speak with her, our conversations would erupt into a shouting match. It appeared that nothing could be done to save our marriage.

After several days, I was able to put my sadness and anger aside to try and make some rational decisions. I decided that it would be best if we at least attempted to save our marriage. Several factors prompted my decision. First of all, there were my children. I remember how much I missed not having a father in my life as a child. I always envied my friends who had fathers, and I remember making a conscious decision to be a good father if I ever had my own children. My children and I were very close, so I definitely wanted to minimize any pain they would experience. Another reason that I thought it would be best to stay together was financial. I knew that if we were to divorce, it would be extremely difficult for me to make it on my own while paying child support and possibly maintaining two households since my wife was a stay-at-home mom. Last but not least (and I'm not proud of this), I was really afraid of what my friends and employees would think of me. In their eyes, I had a perfect life. I had created this image of having it all together, and the thought of going through with this divorce would shatter that image. That really scared me and filled me with shame and embarrassment.

I convinced my wife to try marriage counseling. I told her that I wanted to try and work things out, so we should at least give it a try. She agreed, and we began counseling. After several sessions, it became obvious that our marriage was not going to work out. I discovered that I wanted out of the marriage but was too afraid to say it. All the reasons that I tried to make the marriage work were wrong. I never asked myself the two most important questions of my life: 1. Do I really love her? 2. Do I really want to spend the rest of my life with her? As a result of our counseling, I realized that the answer was "No" to both questions.

Once we knew that the divorce was inevitable, I decided to make it as amicable as possible. I sat down with her and said we should try to make this as simple and painless as possible. Fortunately, she agreed, and we were able to decide how our possessions would be divided up. We were even able to work out visitation with the children. Our divorce was so amicable that we used the same attorney to handle the divorce (if you are currently going through a divorce, I suggest that you do everything in your power to separate on good terms. Although this is extremely difficult, I can assure you that if you put your ego aside and try and work things out together, everybody wins in the end). I must admit that I am truly grateful to my ex-wife for being willing to work things out the way we did. I am forever indebted to her for never speaking badly to our children about me and ensuring that we worked together as parents to help our children handle the whole ordeal. Our willingness to work together to raise our children has paid off with three emotionally and psychologically well-adjusted children that we are both extremely proud of.

After the divorce was final, I found myself in unknown territory. This was actually the first time I had really failed at anything so major and life-changing. I did not know what to expect, but intuitively I knew that I would get through it. At the time, I was somewhat isolated and alone. I did not have any close friends to talk to, so I kept to myself and tried to handle it alone. One of the first declarations I made was never to get married again. Marriage was a difficult and painful experience, and I concluded that I did not want to experience the pain and loss of divorce again. To avoid the potential pain of relationships, I immersed myself in my work

After a few months, I decided to break out of my isolation and at least start going out again. Although I wasn't looking for a relationship, I did at least want to have some companionship.

The problem with going out was that I was still ashamed and embarrassed because of my divorce, and I felt as if I had this huge neon letter 'D' stamped on my forehead. My feelings of inadequacy and failure made it extremely difficult to connect with anyone, so most of the time, I simply went to clubs and danced a little without having many conversations.

Within approximately six months, I started to long for a relationship. I was tired of being alone and missed having a partner to share life with. I decided to try and date to see what would happen. My first few relationships after my divorce were disasters. Although I did not know this then, I was terrified of intimacy. I had all sorts of trouble connecting on an emotional level with women because I was still scarred emotionally from my divorce. After several failures, I began to recognize a pattern in my relationships. I first noticed that my relationships never lasted more than 3-4 weeks. Within that period, something would happen that would terminate the relationship. In most cases, the women were the ones who were saying that they weren't ready for a relationship. If they weren't leaving, I was the one making excuses about why I needed to end the relationship. I had devised some pretty good excuses for ending relationships, like being too busy at work or trying to be a good father to my children. Still, the truth was that I was terrified of experiencing the pain I had associated with relationships.

Prioritize Relationships

After a couple of years, I met a woman that I enjoyed being with. We had great chemistry and a lot in common. After dating her for over a year, I began having deep feelings for her and decided that I wanted to commit to an exclusive relationship with her. When I told her how I felt, her response surprised me. She told me that she liked me a lot and would like to develop a committed relationship with me, but she knew that I was emotionally unavailable to her, so she did not want to invest her feelings into a guy that could not reciprocate her love. I felt rejected and angry and did not know how to respond to her comment. As a result, the relationship ended, and there I was, alone again.

The good news is that I listened to what she had to say. I recognized that I was the problem, not her. I was able to see that I was the reason my relationships weren't working out, and I decided to do something about it. I began my own inner journey to heal my heart so that I would no longer keep pushing women out of my life. I followed M. Scott Peck's advice and took the road less traveled, and I definitely became a better man as a result of it.

After being on my fifteen-year personal journey and learning to love myself, I decided I wanted to remarry. Since I took the time to understand the how's and the why's of my past relationship failures, I was finally able to create loving and supportive relationships without the fear of intimacy or abandonment. As a result of my commitment to my own personal growth, I was able to create a relationship that works for me, which ultimately resulted in me getting remarried and creating a marriage that nurtures and supports me. I enjoy the emotional security that comes from having a spouse that loves and adores me, and I'm truly grateful that I took the time to understand the importance of having authentic relationships.

Great relationships take effort and commitment, but ultimately they are definitely life's greatest treasure. If you have difficulty with relationships, been through or are going through a divorce, or have a deep fear of commitment, take the time to heal your heart, which will open the door to creating great relationships.

Good luck!

"I define spirituality as the moment-to-moment recognition and acknowledgment of my connection to a power greater than myself."
– Coach Michael Taylor

Chapter 8

How Do You See God?

It is arguably the most important question a human being can ask themselves, yet, I believe very few people ever find a complete answer to it.

Does God really exist?

For most of my young life, I was extremely skeptical about the existence of God. I had so many unanswered questions it was difficult for me to truly believe God existed. As a grownup, I lost all faith in organized religion and God and became an Atheist. One thing that fueled my skepticism was the fact that America is one of the most religious countries in the world that was built on the Judea-Christian religion, and yet it is also one of the most violent countries in the world, especially when it came to the treatment of black people.

I remember being approximately ten years old when I walked up to my grandfather and asked him why God was so mad at black people. I was born during the civil rights movement and remember seeing the stories of lynching and police brutality. I wondered why Jesus never did anything to help black people. When I asked my grandfather the question, his reply was, "God isn't mad at black people." He said God had a plan, and that plan was perfect, and even though we may not understand it, we had to accept God's perfect plan.

Even as a child, I could not wrap my mind around that answer. It simply made no sense to me. This was when my skepticism about God began. As I grew up and started to apply rational and critical thinking to the world around me, I focused my attention on science, which is another reason I became an Atheist.

I love science because I love understanding how things work. I've always been very curious and open-minded, and if I didn't know how to do something or understand something, I would always do my research to figure out how to do it or figure out how something worked.

Initially, I tried to apply science to answer my questions about God, but applying science didn't work. It only fueled my skepticism about God. To sum it up, God simply didn't make sense to me based on the teachings of organized religion. It was illogical and irrational.

After being an Atheist for approximately three years, I decided to do more research to try and find some answers to my questions about God. I studied all the major religions and eventually changed my heart about God. During my research, I figured out why I had difficulty believing in God. All of my life, I was trying to "figure out" God in my head instead of trying to find God in my heart. When I learned to open my heart and look for the kingdom within, I found exactly what I was looking for. God wasn't someone "out there." God was something "in here" inside of my heart, and I had to learn to feel the love of God rather than think about God with my intellect to figure out how God worked.

As a result of my search, I was able to create an indescribable intimacy and connection to God. I now describe God as the Divine Intelligence that created and is still creating this amazing Universe we live in. It is this Divine Intelligence that drives me, and it is the foundation of my spirituality.

As a former Atheist, I remember how frustrating it was to listen to people who were trying to ram their religious beliefs down my throat. They believed their beliefs were the right ones, and if I didn't believe in them, I couldn't be a part of their religion. I believe this is one of the primary reasons so many people are turned off to organized religion.

But I believe you can develop intimacy and connection to God without organized religion if you choose to. So my intention isn't to try and convince you there is a God. I intend to ask you a simple question: "How do you see God?"

How Do You See God?

I want to share a chapter from my book, What If Jesus Were A Coach? (www.jesuswasacoach.com) The chapter is titled: How Do You See God? It was written to help you uncover what you really believe about God, and I'm certain it will answer some of the questions you may have about God.

Be sure to read it with an open heart and an open mind, and I'm certain it will provide you with some insights to help you find your truth about God.

Growing up as a child, I remember the picture of Jesus hanging up in my grandparents' home. It was the familiar picture of the white Jesus with a light emanating from his heart, symbolizing his love for humanity. I also remember the Jesus nailed on the cross wall hanging sculpture which also hung on their walls. Even as a child, I didn't understand why Jesus was white and why he hated black people so much.

My grandparents were extremely religious, even though they never went to church. As I mentioned in the previous chapter, they forced me to attend church, yet they never attended. This definitely caused some major conflicts in my mind because even though they talked a lot about Jesus, their actions did not reflect Jesus' teachings. My grandmother was a raging alcoholic who physically and verbally abused me. How could I follow Jesus when the grownup responsible for raising me was such a terrible person?

On the other hand, my grandfather was a quiet gentleman who was deeply religious and filled with wisdom. Even though he only had an eighth-grade education, he was one of the smartest men I've ever known. Some of my fondest memories from childhood were of having conversations with him just about anything. We would sit outside in the yard amongst a myriad of farm animals, and he would share stories about a wide variety of topics, including life. Even though I was just a kid, he talked to me as though I was much older and challenged me to always think about things very deeply.

One day, I asked him why God was so angry at black people. This was during the civil rights movement as I watched news stories of black people being attacked by dogs, sprayed with fire hoses, and beaten by cops. My young ten-year-old mind couldn't understand why black people were maltreated. So in my mind, I concluded that black people must have done something really bad since Jesus didn't step in and stop the abuse black people endured.

When I asked the question, he picked up on the sadness and fear in my voice, and he lifted me and placed me on his knee. He then told me that God wasn't angry at black people. He said that God had a perfect plan, and even though we may not fully understand it, God's plan was perfect. But how could God's plan be so perfect while black people were being so mistreated? He told me not to worry and to trust God's divine plan.

How Do You See God?

As a ten-year-old, I couldn't fully understand what he meant. I tried to rationalize how God's plan was perfect, but I just couldn't see it. In retrospect, and as an adult now, I can definitely understand the perfection of the plan he was talking about. Still, it has taken me years of deep self-introspection and research to fully grasp the implications of what my grandfather told me.

I'm reminded of Albert Einstein's quote, "If you can't explain your subject to an eighth-grader, you don't fully understand your topic." With that being said, I'd like to share how I now see God and how I came to my understanding.

First, I think most people see God as this anthropomorphic being that resides in heaven somewhere. Since most people in the West are Christians, they have this common view that God is some old guy in the clouds who is taking notes of their lives and waiting for them to "sin" so he can banish them to eternal damnation in a fiery hell. This is one of the greatest erroneous-filled teachings of most organized western religions. The error is thinking and believing that God is a human being just like us. Since God is just like us, he must have human emotions and needs, and therefore organized religions have built an entire theology based on the idea that God acts like a human. Why else would he create the ten commandments? Why else would we have to prove our love for him so he wouldn't punish us? Does it make sense to you that an omniscient and omnipresent God would get angry at you for making mistakes? Does it make sense to you that God is a jealous God? These things do not make sense to me, which is why I've always had an issue with organized religion.

The reason most people see God as a human being can be traced to Genesis 1:27, which says, "So God created man in his own image, in the image of God he created him; male and female he created them." This verse has been misinterpreted, and most religions have concluded that this passage implies that God looks like a human being. But if you read John 4:24, it should clarify who and what God is. It says, "God is spirit, and his worshipers must worship in the Spirit and in truth."

As it says, "God is spirit," and since we were made in the image and after the likeness of God, that means we are spirit also.

According to Dr. Wayne Dyer (author and spiritual teacher), we are not human beings having a spiritual experience; we are spiritual beings having a human experience. If you can embrace this idea, rest assured this book will make a lot more sense.

Since most people see Jesus as the personification of God in human form, they have accepted this erroneous belief that God must think and act just like a human being. This is the origin of most conflicts in the world. Believing that God is a "who" instead of a "what." I believe that God is the Divine Intelligence that created and is still creating this amazing Universe we live in. Therefore, I see God as more of a "what" than a "who." Seeing God this way answers another question I had as a child. Where was God before the Universe began?

To answer that question, let's begin by listening to two of the most brilliant men and greatest minds the world has ever seen.

Albert Einstein once said, "Everything is energy, that's just the way that it is. Match the frequency of the reality you want to create and there is no way you can't create that reality. It can be no other way. This isn't philosophy, this is physics."

Nikola Tesla said, "If you want to understand the Universe, you must think in terms of energy, frequency, and vibration."

Both of these brilliant minds point to a scientific fact. Everything is energy!

So, where did this energy come from? This is the million-dollar question!

To answer it, you have three options.

Option 1. It was a random act that just happened. Option 2. Something caused it to happen. Option 3. You do not know where it came from.

Option number one is based on science. Science says a Big Bang occurred randomly, and the Universe is the result of a chemical reaction that evolved into our current Universe.

Option number two is based on a belief that a Creator caused the Universe to take form. Every religion is based on this option.

Option number three is, "I really do not know!"

So which option best describes what you believe, Option #1, Option #2, or Option #3?

To help you choose which option you believe in, let's go back several thousand years. Try to imagine what it must have been like to be a caveman. During that time, your primary responsibility was to provide food and shelter for you and your family and protect yourself and your family from being eaten alive by dinosaurs. For the most part, it was a pretty simple life. You didn't have language but learned to communicate with pictures and sounds. As cave dwellers evolved, they developed language and learned to make weapons and basic tools for their survival. As they continued to evolve, they realized certain things that they didn't understand or have control over, so they came up with stories and ideas to try and make sense of natural phenomena. For example, if lightning struck, they had no idea where the lightning came from, so they created stories to explain where it originated.

They then came up with the idea that some sort of powerful force in the sky was shooting lightning bolts at them. If they contracted a disease, they created stories that said the gods up in the sky were angry and were punishing them for one reason or another. So, man's lack of understanding of the physical world around them caused them to come up with explanations of things they didn't understand. Therefore, these stories became religions.

As these stories were passed down from generation to generation, human beings were still evolving. Some significantly evolved beings began teaching that there was a Creator of all things, and they provided some new stories about how this Creator operated. These evolved beings laid the groundwork for all religions, and their teachings spread across the globe.

The problem, as I see it, was each of these evolved beings shared a message of oneness with the Creator. However, each evolved being had their own unique interpretation of what the Creator was expecting from human beings, and they shared their "truth" with the masses, and then the masses started sharing those truths with others. Unfortunately, many of the evolved being's messages got lost in translation and were misinterpreted and even completely changed. Yet, the masses concluded that their evolved being was the chosen evolved being, and if you didn't follow their evolved being's way of worshipping God, you could not be a part of their evolved being's tribe. So, each tribe believed their evolved being was teaching the "right" way to connect with God, and the other evolved beings were teaching the "wrong" way of connecting with God.

Therefore, religion is a belief in a story of an evolved being that came to teach human beings how to connect to the

Creator. The downside of religion is that they promote exclusivity. If you do not believe in their teachings, you are seen as different and separate from that particular group. In other words, if you do not believe in what they believe, you cannot be a part of their tribe. This is the core essence of religion.

On the other hand, you have spirituality. Spirituality suggests that several evolved beings have walked the earth, and each one shared the same message. Their primary message is that there is a Divine Creator of the Universe, and every human being has equal access to this Creator. Being spiritual but not religious means recognizing that all religions originate from the same source and lead to the same place. Therefore, you accept that some people may believe in a different God other than yours, but that doesn't mean they can't be a part of your tribe. Spirituality is all-inclusive and welcomes all human beings into one Universal tribe.

There was a time when I believed in option #1. As I mentioned earlier, I concluded there was no such thing as God, and I held firm to the belief that science had the answer to everything, and if it couldn't be proved by science, it simply wasn't real. But then, I made a paradigm shift. I changed my rigid way of thinking by researching the different religions and coming to my own conclusions and beliefs about God.

To provide you with some fuel for contemplation, I'd like to share some things I've learned that confirm that science and spirituality go together. I realize that some people may not believe this, but I will assume you are open-minded enough to believe what I am about to share since you're still reading.

Let's go back to the quote, "everything is energy." There is a scientific process called reductionism, which means you can take anything and reduce it down to its smallest component to know exactly what it is made of. At a time, scientists thought the smallest particle of matter was the atom, so they concluded that the atom was the building block of all matter. As science evolved and technology increased, they realized the atom wasn't the smallest particle of matter. When they broke down everything into its smallest component, they realized that everything was actually composed of energy. In other words, nothing is actually solid. It's energy vibrating at different speeds, and as this energy slows down, it becomes solid matter. Dr. Joe Dispenza explained it this way, "If you stripped an atom down to its raw essentials, all that exists is energy and information, but the atom is not without design. Even at that quantum level, there is a structure and orderliness, so there must be some intelligence or force unifying and ordering them."

So, what is this intelligence or force, and where did it come from?

Once again, this is the million-dollar question. Did this energy and intelligence randomly appear or did "something" cause it to appear?

As a result of my research, I have come to some conclusions that I would like to share with you. To fully grasp what I'm about to share, it may require you to create a new paradigm on what you believe about how the Universe began.

I'd like you to try to imagine complete darkness and emptiness. Put another way, try to imagine complete nothingness. In this nothingness, nothing exists. There is no light or darkness, or even time. It is pure nothingness. Can you imagine it? Now try to imagine that all of a sudden, something came from nothing. If you believe in science, the instant that something came from nothing was called the Big Bang. If you're religious, it was in that moment that God said, "Let there be light." Either way, the point here is at first, there was nothing, and then there was something. If you choose to see this event from a scientific perspective, how would you explain that? If there was absolute nothingness and then something came from nothing, that means the nothingness was actually something because it would be impossible for something to come from nothing. Are you still with me here? Think deeply about that. How could something come from nothing? I would like to propose that the nothingness is actually something and that something could be called Pure Consciousness or Divine Intelligence. You could even call it Love, which is the highest vibration in the Universe. If you're religious, you can call it God. As I see it, it is the Source of all things. Everything in the Universe arises from this Divine Intelligence. The instant something came from nothing, an energy was released and there is an intelligence that drives this energy. The intelligence that drives this energy is called evolution. Evolution is the process through which Divine Intelligence evolves to deeper and deeper levels of complexity and this is an ongoing process that will continue throughout eternity.

This energy is within you, and true spirituality is developing an intimacy with and connection to this energy. You do not have to be religious to connect to this energy. Even if you do not believe in this energy, it is still there. Each religion is supposed to help you recognize this energy within you. Unfortunately, most religions get caught up in religious dogma and doctrine and fail to teach you the truth about accessing this energy.

This answers my question of where was God before the Universe began. God was everywhere because God is everything. If God were a human being, where would he/she have been before the Universe began? Hmmm?

I do not believe we can fully grasp exactly what God is in our limited human minds. Choosing to see God as Love, Divine Intelligence, or Pure Consciousness it allows us to grasp the idea of God and yet it doesn't fully explain what God truly is. It's like trying to imagine how long eternity is. Eternity is forever. It never stops. So is God; it is everything and nothing at the same time. It doesn't come to an end.

Now that I've shared how I see God, I'd like to share another thing I've learned about God and the Holy Trinity. Have you ever had someone try to explain the Holy Trinity to you? The Trinity states that there is The Father, The Son, and The Holy Spirit, yet they are all supposed to be the same thing. How is that possible? This is incredibly confusing, and I definitely had difficulty understanding it based on traditional Christianity, so I would like to share my perception of the Holy Trinity.

To start, let's take a look at Genesis Chapter 1, verse 26. "Then God said, "Let us make man in our image, in our likeness, and let them rule over the fish of the sea and the birds of the air, over the livestock, over all the earth and over all the creatures that move along the ground."

Let me preface this explanation with a little caveat. I do not believe in the literal interpretation of the bible. I believe in the metaphysical interpretation. This means the stories in the bible are metaphorical, allegorical, and not written to be taken literally but to be understood spiritually and metaphorically. Therefore, each story allows us to learn something about ourselves to help us grow into the best version of ourselves.

One question I could never get a minister to answer was based on that quote from Genesis 1:26. Why did God say, "Let "us" make man in "our" image?" Who was he referring to when he said that? Why didn't he say let me make man in my image?

I've never had anyone explain this to me, so I'm certain someone reading this has the same question, so now I'd like to share my answer.

How Do You See God?

Let's go back to the beginning. Remember when I said there was nothing, and then all of a sudden, there was something? The nothingness was God or Pure Consciousness. The instant something came from nothing, something was "born." That something that was born could be referred to as energy. Since the bible was written by men from a patriarchal point of view, we use the term "Father," but in reality, "Mother" would have been more appropriate since men do not give birth, but for the sake of this discussion, we will leave that alone. So, the "Father," which is God or Divine Intelligence, gave birth to an energy that we will call its son. If you practice Christianity, you would call this son Christ. If you follow the Tao, you would call this son Chi, and if you're Native American, you would call this son Catori. Regardless of what you call it, it is an energy that originated from the Father or Creator. So now you have the father and the son, but what about the Holy Spirit? The Holy Spirit is the individual expression of the son.

Think of it this way. There is a spark of divinity in every human being. You have it, I have it, everyone has it. This spark, this energy, is divine, and it is your birthright. This spark, which was birthed by the Father and expressed by the son, needed a way to be expressed, so God created man/woman to be the divine expression of itself.

Here is a simple story to illustrate what I mean.

Once upon a time, God was sitting up in heaven looking down at the earth at human beings with a few of his angels when he became overwhelmed with pride. "Human beings are without question my greatest creations. I want to give them something that I didn't give to any other creatures on earth; I want to give them a part of me. But I don't want to just give it to them; I want them to earn it so they will truly appreciate this divine gift. So, I need to figure out a place to put it where they will have to put forth some effort to find it. Where do you think I should put it?

One of the angels spoke up and said, "I know where you can put it. Why not put it on top of the tallest mountain? God thought about it for a moment, and then he said, "I don't think that's a good idea. Human beings will easily climb the highest mountain and find this gift."

Then another angel spoke up, "I know where to hide it. Why not put it at the bottom of the ocean? Surely it would be difficult for man to find it there."

Once again, God thought about it and said, "I don't think so. Human beings are naturally curious, and I don't think they would have any problems finding it at the bottom of the ocean."

Then another angel spoke up, "Why not place it amongst the stars? Surely human beings would find it difficult to find it among the stars."

God pondered the idea for a moment and responded the same way. "Human beings are ingenious and adventurous. I don't think it would be hard for them to find it among the stars.

Then another angel walked up to God and said, "I know the perfect place for you to hide it. I am certain it would be the last place human beings would ever look. Why not put your divine spark inside of them?"

All of a sudden, a huge smile came across God's face. "That is brilliant! What a great idea. I agree with you totally, so I will place my divine spark inside of every human being, and it will be up to them to find it."

This story serves as a perfect metaphor for what the Holy Spirit is. It is a divine spark of God that gives us access to God in our own unique individual way, and it is our responsibility to find it. No one can find it for us.

One of my favorite quotes is, "If you don't go within, you will always go without." Therefore, if you are unwilling to look within your own heart and mind, you will never find God. Most religions have promoted the idea that God is somewhere outside of you, but the truth is, God has always been inside of you.

Going back to the story I shared about God looking down on earth at human beings and being proud of his creations, God came up with the perfect plan to find a way to express itself on earth. In Genesis 1:27, it says, "So God created man in his own image, in the image of God he created him; male and female he created them." Verse 28 says, "God blessed them and said to them: Be fruitful and multiply; fill the earth and subdue it.

Rule over the fish of the sea and the birds of the air and over every living creature that moves on the ground."

The way I interpret those two verses is, God made it clear that human beings were its greatest creation. They were given a divine part of God, and therefore, they had dominion over all other creations. Looking at it from a metaphysical perspective, human beings are divine individual expressions of God.

Think of it this way.

Take a moment and think about the ocean. If you stand on a beach and look toward the horizon, it looks infinite, it looks beautiful, it looks powerful, and it looks majestic. Now imagine that you have a jar, and you walk to the ocean and scoop up a jar of ocean. The jar of ocean has the exact same qualities, characteristics, and attributes of the ocean. It is, in fact, the ocean. There is no difference. But can the jar of ocean be the ocean in its totality? No! It is an individual expression of the ocean, but it cannot be the entire ocean. And yet, there is absolutely no difference.

This is another way to see God. God is the ocean, and you are an individual expression of God. You have all of the same qualities, characteristics, and attributes of God, but you could never be God in its totality.

Put another way, you are a divine personality in the mind of God. As personalities in the mind of God, God communicates with us through divine ideas. Ideas are the currency of the

How Do You See God?

Universe, and when you learn to quiet the noise of your mind and move into the silence of your heart, then you will hear the voice of your soul, which are the divine ideas that come directly from God. I'll be sharing more about this in the next chapter.

I'd like to close this chapter with a very important question. As a matter of fact, it's possibly the most important question you've ever been asked. So when I ask the question, I want you to take a moment and truly think about it before you answer. Spend some time in deep contemplation, and then answer the question as honestly as you can. Try not to allow other people's opinions or what you have been taught to believe to influence your answer. Listen to your own heart and mind and answer truthfully. No one needs to know your answer except you.

Are you ready?

What are your beliefs about God?

Notice I didn't ask you if you believe in God; I asked what your beliefs about God are. For some people, they may not believe God exists. For other people, they may have a very strong belief in God. Some may believe in an anthropomorphic god sitting in heaven, taking notes of their lives and waiting for them to die to see if they can get into heaven. Others may believe in a God of love who loves them unconditionally, accepts them with open, loving arms, and showers them with grace.

So if you truly want to know what type of God you believe in, let me suggest you simply take a deep look at your life right now, and you will find your answer. Always remember, your belief about a thing creates your experience of that thing. If you believe in an angry, judgmental God to whom you have to repent of your sins to try and get into heaven, chances are your life is filled with fear and anxiety. On the other hand, if you believe in a God of love, your life could be filled with joy, inner peace, and happiness.

But ultimately, your beliefs about God will always create your experience of God, so it's important to be really clear about what you believe. I am convinced most people really do not know what they believe about God. They may know what they were taught to believe about God through their families and cultures, but they have never really questioned or challenged those beliefs. They have simply accepted beliefs that may have been passed down for generations, and they are convinced that their beliefs are the "right" beliefs and that anyone who doesn't believe what they believe is "wrong."

It is now up to you to decide how you see God. I hope this chapter has provided you with some fuel for contemplation and some insights that will support you in creating an intimate connection to a power greater than yourself.

Rest assured, when you do, your life will become miraculous!

"Everything is energy and that's all there is to it. Match the frequency of the reality you want and you cannot help but get that reality. It can be no other way. This is not philosophy. This is physics."
- Albert Einstein

Chapter 9

Spiritual Laws and Principles

I would like for you to take a moment to read the quote below.

"You are more than your thoughts, your body, or your feelings. You are a swirling vortex of limitless potential who is here to shake things up and create something new that the Universe has never seen."

As you read the quote, what thoughts came to mind? How did you feel after reading it? Did you feel excited? Scared? Confused? Uncertain? What if the quote is true? What if I told you that you are an unlimited being with infinite potential?

Would you believe me?

Unfortunately, most people wouldn't. But the fact that you are reading this book right now tells me that you are not "most

Spiritual Laws and Principles

people." If you are the type of person who reads a book like this, that tells me that you are open-minded, curious, and willing to learn and grow, and therefore it's quite possible that you believe the quote. You've probably already agreed with it and are now ready to create something new that the Universe has never seen - so let's just jump right in and get started.

The truth is, an overwhelming majority of people do not believe the quote. They will accept societally-driven labels that define who they are without asking themselves deeper questions like "who am I, and why am I here?" This chapter is designed to give you some insights on possibly answering those two questions. Are you ready to answer those questions for yourself?

If you ask most people who they are, they will usually respond with answers such as their name, whether they have a family, what they do for a living, if they are a democrat or republican, an African American or Caucasian, a Christian or a Muslim (or are part of a host of other religions), an American or Asian - the list of labels goes on and on. But if you think deeply about this, these are just titles and labels that we use to define who we are. To prove my point, I want you to do a simple test. Walk up to a mirror and ask yourself what you see. Do you see a republican? A Christian? A husband? A manager?

The answer is that you see a human being. The mirror can't lie; it can only reflect what is placed in front of it. All the titles and labels you use to define yourself aren't who you are; they are simply titles, labels, and beliefs you have accepted to define yourself. For example, have you ever known someone who used to be a Republican, but then became a Democrat? Or someone who was a Christian, who then became a Muslim? Or maybe someone who was pro-life, then became pro-choice? If they looked in the mirror as a republican and then became a democrat, what would they see in the mirror? They would see a human being, not a label. Labels are really just beliefs. You are not a label. You are a human being with different beliefs, and although your beliefs may change, you will not.

What you see in the mirror is what you truly are, but it goes a lot deeper than that. What you are, is not necessarily who you are.

Let me explain in more detail.

What you are is a human being with flesh and bones. This is an indisputable fact. But who you are is the divine being that resides within the flesh and bones. Here is another way to look at it - if I stand in front of a mirror and look at myself, I notice that I'm wearing a shirt. So if I say that is "my" shirt, who owns it? I do - it is "my" shirt. Now, I continue to look into the mirror and notice my body. Who is the "me" that owns the body? If this is "my" body, who am I? I want to suggest that the "me" that owns the body is actually my spirit. Put another way, you are not actually a human being having a spiritual experience - you are a spiritual being having a human experience, and your body is just like the suit of clothes you are wearing.

If you can wrap your mind around this idea, then the original quote that I began this chapter with should make more sense to you. The quote said, "You are a swirling vortex of limitless potential who is here to shake things up and create something new that the Universe has never seen." Which simply means that you are a divine spiritual being expressing yourself through human form. You have unique gifts and talents that must be shared with the world if you truly want to live a rewarding and fulfilling life.

So what do you think? Do you believe this? Can you accept that you are much more than your physical body? Can you embrace the idea that you are a divine spiritual being with unlimited potential who is here to shake things up?

Since you're still reading this book, you're ready to dive deep into who you really are! So let's begin with understanding your divine makeup.

You are actually a three-part being which can be described as body, mind, and spirit. You are a spirit, which is housed in a body that has a mind. Your body is like the clothes you wear, and your mind is like a tool you use to help make conscious decisions and learn new things. They all work in harmony.

The Brothahood of Kings

As a spiritual being, you have an infinite capacity for learning and creativity. There are absolutely no limits to the number of things you can learn and create. Your imagination only limits you, and even your imagination is unlimited.

So, let's break down the three parts of your being. Let's begin with your mind.

It's important that you understand your mind and how it works if you truly want to discover who you are. I'll begin by saying that the mind and the brain are not really the same thing. Your brain is the organ that serves as the center of your nervous system and is responsible for cognitive thinking and memory. In my opinion, it is the most amazing organ in your body, and it works just like a muscle - the more you use it, the stronger it gets.

The mind, however, is separate and distinct from the brain, although they work together. It is almost impossible to truly define the mind. Scientists have been trying to define it in scientific terms for millennia, but unfortunately, there has never been a consensus on exactly what the mind is. Rather than try to argue and define it, I will simply share a definition that I truly resonate with, and it is this definition I will use to explain what I believe the mind does and how it works.

The mind is "the element of a person that enables them to be aware of the world and their experiences, to think, and to feel; the faculty of consciousness and thought."

Spiritual Laws and Principles

I really like the last part of this definition; the faculty of consciousness and thought.

According to Dr. Bruce Lipton, author of the amazing book The Biology Of Belief, the mind actually has two parts; the conscious mind and the subconscious mind. A great metaphor to explain how it works is an iceberg. If you look at an iceberg in the ocean, you will only see a small portion of it above the water, but did you know that in some cases, 90% of the iceberg is actually below the surface? This is how the mind works. The top 10% is your conscious mind, and the lower 90% is your subconscious mind. What is fascinating is that the subconscious mind is 1000 times more powerful than the conscious mind when it comes to influencing your behavior.

Dr. Lipton explained it this way:

When we are born, we are completely conscious of all the external stimuli that we interact with. As children, we process primarily through our feelings without judgment or thought about the situation. In other words, we use our hearts, not our minds, to interpret everything around us. Our feelings become the guidepost of our experiences.

During the first 7-10 years of our lives, our subconscious mind works like a video recorder. It simply records all the external events in our lives, and then it begins associating feelings, memories, and beliefs with those events. As we grow older, we begin to form subconscious beliefs about everything we come into contact with. As we form these beliefs, we then begin making assumptions about who we are and how we fit into the world. Our prerecorded tapes become our subconscious beliefs about ourselves, and everything we think and do is then filtered through and influenced by these prerecorded tapes.

So take a moment to think about your own childhood, especially between when you were born and when you turned seven. What do you remember? Do you remember growing up in a loving, caring home, or was it one filled with violence and dysfunction?

Whether you realize it or not, your childhood strongly impacts your behavior, even as an adult. If you remember being loved and nurtured as a child, the chances are your subconscious mind is filled with positive beliefs about yourself. In other words, your prerecorded tapes are positive, which in most cases means you will feel good about yourself and have a positive attitude about life. On the other hand, if you remember pain and misery growing up, there is a good chance that your prerecorded tapes about yourself may be negative, which in turn may cause you to create a negative outlook on life.

You can look at the subconscious mind as a big memory bank that stores your beliefs, memories, and life experiences. All your thoughts are instantly processed through your subconscious beliefs. Look at it this way - once your subconscious tapes are programmed during your childhood, every thought and action you have as an adult will be based on the programming you experienced growing up.

On the other hand, you have your conscious mind, which could be referred to as your "intellect." The conscious mind is where you store information that you have learned through rigorous study and learning. When you go to school and learn facts, you are using your conscious mind. When you calculate and figure out solutions to most problems, you are also using your conscious mind, but remember what I said about the subconscious mind being 1000 times more powerful than the conscious mind?

Here is an example of how this works.

Imagine that you know someone that has a Ph.D. in astrophysics. This person is obviously extremely intelligent and has a highly-developed conscious mind. But imagine too that this person has difficulty creating healthy relationships. No matter what they do, they always experience difficulty in relationships. Why do you think this is? They are obviously very smart, yet they can't figure out how to make relationships work. Why is that?

Well, it's actually pretty simple. On a conscious level, they can read a book about relationships and explain to you intellectually how relationships work, which uses the conscious mind. But their subconscious is 1000 times more powerful than their conscious mind, so when they enter into a relationship, the subconscious beliefs they have about themselves will always override the conscious mind. No matter how many books they read or how smart they are, if they have deeply rooted negative subconscious beliefs about themselves, they will never be able to create healthy relationships.

This is why it is so important to understand how the mind works. No matter how much we may learn on a conscious level, if we aren't willing to look at our subconscious beliefs, we can never truly change our lives. We each have deeply held subconscious beliefs about a wide variety of things, and until we become willing to change these subconscious beliefs, we will not be able to overcome our subconscious conditioning.

Let's take a look at some subconscious beliefs that may be sabotaging your life right now.

Are you currently struggling financially and can't figure out why? Well, there is a very good chance that your subconscious beliefs are actually keeping you from being financially secure. If you grew up hearing that money was the root of all evil or that rich people were stuck up and selfish, you may have subconscious beliefs that keep you from making a lot of money because your subconscious belief might be that money is "bad."

If you're a man and you struggle with relationships, you may have subconscious beliefs that say women only want you for your money or women can't be trusted. This belief will eventually sabotage any new relationship you enter. If you're a woman struggling with relationships, then it's quite possible that you have subconscious beliefs that all men are dogs and only want sex. Therefore this belief will keep you from creating true intimacy with men because of your lack of trust. If you happen to be religious, you may have subconscious beliefs that you are a sinner, and there is nothing you can do except repent of your sins and hope that God forgives you for being a sinner.

No matter what subconscious beliefs you have, you must understand that those subconscious beliefs are actually the cause of most of the pain, suffering, and lack of experience you have in life. To sum it up, your subconscious beliefs create your reality, so if you aren't happy with any area of your life right now, I can assure you that the main reason is that you have some unconscious belief that is causing you pain and misery.

It is absolutely imperative that you begin examining your deeply held subconscious beliefs if you truly want to change, but rest assured that it is possible for you to do so.

Now that you have a deeper understanding of how the subconscious mind works, here's the good news: when you realize just how powerful the mind really is, you can use it to create anything you want.

Have you ever heard this quote: "Whatever the mind can conceive, you can achieve, if you really believe?"

Do you believe it? Is it really possible?

I believe the answer is "yes," and now I would like to share how and why this is possible. So let's go back to the definition I posted earlier: The mind is "the element of a person that enables them to be aware of the world and their experiences, to think, and to feel; the faculty of consciousness and thought."

I want you to focus on "the faculty of consciousness and thought."

Here is another way to look at it. Try to imagine there is a Divine Intelligence that permeates the Universe. This Intelligence is the Source of all things. It is inherent in all things. It keeps the planets aligned and causes a seed to grow into a flower. The same intelligence causes a bone to heal and the earth to orbit the sun.

There are many different names for this Source, but the name does not matter. You can call it God, The Creator, Yahweh, Jehovah, Great Spirit, The Universe, or any other name, but what is most important is that you believe and trust that it is available to you (throughout this book, I will simply refer to it as The

Source). You do not have to believe in any particular religion or dogma to have access to it. You must simply open your heart and your mind to the truth that it exists. If you accept this truth, you must accept that your mind is connected to The Source. Your mind is like a conduit through which The Source allows divine intelligence to flow to you and through you.

Now you must remember what I said at the beginning. The mind and the brain are not the same thing. The brain can only process information that you have provided to it. The brain is not creative - it is not the source of imagination, creativity, or divine ideas. The brain is also not the source of inspiration or insight; these are all functions of the mind, which can also be referred to as the heart or the center of your being.

Author and spiritual teacher Iyanla Vanzant said, "The mind is a powerful, creative energy. Everything we think, do, and feel begins in the mind. For this reason, we have to address the thoughts, beliefs, judgments, learnings, and perceptions that we hold in our minds."

The reason the quote "whatever the mind can conceive you can achieve" is true is because The Source of all things is purely creative, and it needs you to co-create with it. So when your mind conceives a divine idea from The Source, which is all-powerful and limitless, you can accomplish it if you're willing to work hand-in-hand with The Source and put forth a lot of effort to bring it to fruition.

The Brothahood of Kings

One of my favorite spiritual teachers is Deepak Chopra. He shared a very powerful quote that really speaks to this truth. He said: "Inherent in every intention and desire are the mechanics for its fulfillment." Put another way, The Source will not give you an idea you can't accomplish. The Source knows exactly what you're capable of and will only give you divine ideas that are attainable for you. You wouldn't even have the idea in the first place if you weren't capable of accomplishing it.

As I mentioned previously, the mind is the source of imagination and is the key to creating anything you want in life. Let me share a brief story with you to validate my point.

During the darkest period of my life, I was deeply depressed and unsure of how I would get my life back on track. At the time, I had no money, job, relationship, or material possessions, and things seemed pretty hopeless. But the one thing I did have was my imagination, and I began to use it to help me change my situation. Despite having absolutely nothing, I began imagining my life getting better. Instead of focusing on all the things I didn't have, I focused on what I did have. I would begin each day counting my blessings for everything I had, such as my health, ability to learn, positive attitude, a few close friends, children who loved me, and the fact that I was even alive.

I began envisioning what my life would be like once I got back on my feet, and I somehow knew that, eventually, I would. As

Spiritual Laws and Principles

I continued to focus on the things I did have and on the future that I wanted to create, things slowly started to change for me. Eventually, I found a job, then I purchased a car, and finally, I was able to get my own apartment. Although this took a couple of years, my point is that I used my imagination to see the things I wanted, and then I worked hard to get them. It all began in my mind. I had to be willing to use my mind and imagination before creating the things I wanted.

As I think back in retrospect, I can now see how The Source was the source of all of the ideas I used to put my life back together. It was The Source that would provide me with ideas on where to look for employment and gave me the inspiration to remain positive even when I had nothing. It was The Source that gave me the strength and courage to move through all of my life's challenges without giving up and falling victim to despair. It was The Source that encouraged me and helped me to focus on my ultimate destiny, and it didn't allow me to quit.

Even through those difficult times, I held on to my dreams of becoming a successful entrepreneur, writer, and speaker one day. I had no evidence that I could do these things; I only had the belief and faith that I could. Belief and faith originate in the mind, and I now recognize that each originates from The Source.

And now, here I am, some thirty years later, doing exactly what I imagined I would be doing. All because I believe that you can achieve whatever the mind can conceive.

It's important that you understand I am no different than you are. I am a divine spiritual being with direct access to The Source, and so are you. You have a mind and direct access to The Source. There is nothing you cannot accomplish if you choose to access your divinity, but it is up to you to go a little deeper and figure out what negative subconscious beliefs you may have about yourself and change them. It is your responsibility to learn more about your mind and begin using it to create the life you deserve. So, now let's talk about your body.

I believe that the human body is the most amazing thing on this planet. I do not believe that there is anything more miraculous. Although most people take their bodies for granted, I believe it is the greatest gift that The Source provided us with. I mentioned earlier that the body is simply a suit of clothing that your spirit wears, so I must admit that The Source knew exactly what it was doing when it created the human body. Of course, everyone is aware of their own physical body, but did you know that you also have an emotional or energetic body?

If you accept the fact that you are a spiritual being, then it makes it easier to grasp how the emotional/energetic body works.

Think of it this way:

Imagine that you have an opening in the top of your skull, and a pipe goes from the top of your skull to the bottom of your belly. This pipe flows with energy that comes directly from The Source; this energy is your life force and permeates your entire being. When you are born, the pipe is completely open, allowing Source energy to flow through you easily. This energy causes you to feel alive and connected to life. This energy is then converted into feelings, which is the spirit's way of communicating with the body. There are primarily four energies that move throughout the energetic body: joy, anger, sadness, and fear.

As a child, whenever you experienced one of these feelings, you acted appropriately and expressed the feeling through an emotion. For example, if you felt sad, you would cry; if you felt angry, you would scream or lash out; if you felt joy, you would smile and laugh; and if you felt fear, you would close off or retreat. As long as you express the feeling appropriately, the energetic pipe stays open and clear, and your life force energy continues to flow through you.

As you grow older, your parents or family members begin conditioning you to believe that expressing them is wrong, so what happens is you begin to repress and suppress your feelings, and each time you do, you begin to create little energy blocks in the pipe. It's like building up plaque in your arteries. The more you suppress your feelings, the more the energetic pipe clogs up, and before you know it, the pipe is completely closed and you are cut off from your life force. When this happens, you lose your sense of aliveness because the divine flow of energy has been cut off. Once the flow of energy has been cut off and we have been disconnected from The Source, we then learn to process everything through our conscious mind or intellect, and we become very rational and analytical. In other words, we try to rely on our brains instead of our minds and hearts.

The bad news is the energetic body works like the subconscious mind. We may not be aware of it, but our repressed emotions sometimes cause us to act out irrationally because we are completely unconscious of the pain we may be carrying. Here is a good example. Have you ever met someone or know someone who is always angry? No matter what is going on, this person is angry and negative, and they usually aren't that pleasant to be around. They get angry and upset at the slightest provocation, and no matter what you say or do, they will negatively respond to just about everything. Do you know anyone like that? Are you like that?

Why do you think this person acts this way? It's because they have trapped emotional energy in their emotional body, and until they learn how to release it, they will always act out of anger.

On the flip side of that, maybe you know someone who always pretends to be happy. They are the "people pleasing" types who always seek approval and pretend that everything is always okay. The only emotion they express is happiness, but unfortunately, they are completely sad and emotionally bankrupt inside. A person like this usually has trapped anger, fear, or sadness in their emotional bodies, and rather than feel these emotions, they hide behind being happy all the time.

When we have repressed or suppressed emotions, they can sabotage all areas of our lives. As long as we feel and release our feelings appropriately, the life force can move through us, but as we shut down the flow, we create a disconnection from The Source, and it leads to all sorts of problems in our lives.

It's important that you take care of both of your bodies - your physical body and your emotional one. You take care of the physical body by eating the right foods and exercising. You take care of the emotional body by investing in some emotional healing work that allows you to release any repressed energy trapped in your emotional body. Now that you better understand how the mind and the body work together, it's time to fully understand who you really are.

Every major religion promotes a very simple and profound truth. There is a Source through which all things are created. It does not matter which religion you follow as long as you accept this simple fact. This Source is the Divine Intelligence that created and is still creating the Universe, and you have unlimited access to this Source. As a human being, you are a divine expression of this Source, which means that you can co-create anything your heart desires with this Source.

The Brothahood of Kings

Think of it this way - if you look at the ocean, you will see a powerful, beautiful, and seemingly infinite body of water. If you walk up to the ocean and scoop up a small cup of it, what you will have in the cup is ocean. But the cup of ocean could never be the ocean in its totality, so it is a divine expression of the ocean. This expression is no different than the ocean; as a matter of fact, it contains all of the same qualities, characteristics, and attributes of the ocean. It is the ocean in an individualized expression. As long as the expression of the ocean stays connected to the ocean, it will thrive and express exactly the way the ocean does. But if the ocean in the cup is separated from the ocean, eventually, it will dry up and no longer exist as that unique expression.

The Source is just like the ocean. You are an individual expression of the Source. You have the same qualities, characteristics, and attributes as the Source. You are no different from The Source. As long as you stay connected to The Source, you can co-create with it, and since The Source is infinite, so are you.

Do not buy into societal labels and constructs that will convince you that there is something wrong with you. Disregard all labels and titles and come to the understanding that you are a divine spiritual being with unlimited potential, and the only thing that can keep you from accomplishing anything is yourself. This includes letting go of the attachment to your ethnic identity. You should definitely be proud of your ethnic heritage, whatever it may be, but you must understand that your spiritual nature has nothing to do with skin color or nationality. The Source transcends race, and so do you if you accept who and what you truly are.

Titles and labels will only hold you back, but accepting the truth of your being will definitely set you free. Remember that you are three parts being - Spirit, Mind, and Body - connected to The Source, and you can co-create anything your heart desires.

I want to close this chapter with something for you to think about. I would like for you to think about a snowflake.

If you look at snowflakes falling from the sky, they appear to be the same. They all have the same color, texture, and smell. They are all composed of the same stuff and come from the same source. But if you look under a microscope, every snowflake is completely different. No two snowflakes are alike. Just imagine – out of the billions of snowflakes that fall from the sky, none of them are the same.

The truth is, you are just like the snowflake. Out of the seven billion human beings on the planet, there is only one you. When it comes to human beings, The Source never replicates itself. You are a divine, unique individual expression of The Source, and it is your responsibility to accept this fact.

Your job is to come to this understanding and to recognize that you have unlimited potential and you have been given some unique gifts and talents that are yours alone - and your job is to share them with the world. This is why the quote I shared at the beginning of the chapter is so important. It states a divine truth, and I hope you will take it to heart and accept it as your truth.

So I will leave you with that quote, and I hope you will embrace it and accept the truth it shares.

"You are more than your thoughts, your body, or your feelings. You are a swirling vortex of limitless potential who is here to shake things up and create something new that the Universe has never seen."

"If you don't make the commitment today to start becoming the person you need to be to create the extraordinary life you really want, what makes you think that tomorrow - or next week, or next month, or next year - is going to be any different? They won't. And that's why you must draw your line in the sand TODAY." - Hal Elrod

Chapter 10

The Four Pillars Of An Extraordinary Life

I was born in the inner-city projects of Corpus Christi, Texas, to a single mother with six kids. We were basically the poster children for poverty back in the sixties. To say we were poor would be an understatement. I remember my mom working 2-3 jobs at a time just to make ends meet. I remember food stamps and government housing and having to eat soggy fried egg sandwiches for lunch, which I hated.

Despite our financial situation, my mother never conceded to a poverty mindset. She always maintained a positive outlook and attitude and instilled in me the idea that things would always get better. She never complained or blamed anyone for her situation, which instilled a deep sense of self responsibility in me. I learned from an early age that I was responsible for my life turning out the way I wanted it to, and no one could keep me from living my dreams.

The Four Pillars Of An Extraordinary Life

If there is such a thing as an optimist gene, my mother passed it on to me. I have always maintained a positive attitude and my optimistic outlook has allowed me to overcome seemingly insurmountable obstacles in my life.

If I had to sum up the most important lesson my mom taught me, it would be summed up with this simple yet powerful quote from my mom, "If you want something badly enough, there is no one or no thing that can keep you from attaining it except yourself." Even though I was probably six years old when she shared this piece of wisdom, the lesson deeply resonated with me and became the mantra that I've used all of my life to succeed.

Another influential person in my life was my grandfather. He was a quiet, soft-spoken man who always dropped nuggets of wisdom on me. I'll always remember one particular conversation he and I had about me becoming a millionaire. The conversation went something like this:

"Grandfather, when I grow up, I'm going to be rich."

"And how do you plan on doing that?" he asked.

"I'm going to own my own company," I replied.

"Well, that's great, so if that's what you want to do when you grow up, let me give you the secrets to being rich. There are really only two secrets you need to know in order to be rich. I promise that if you remember these two things, there is nothing you can't accomplish. Are you listening?"

The Brothahood of Kings

"Yes, grandfather."

"Well, the first thing you have to do is learn to think like the white man. Now, this doesn't mean you are supposed to try and be something you aren't. Never try and pretend that you are white, and never be ashamed that you are black. That simply means you have to think like a rich person. Since the white man is the one with all the money, you have to think the way he does. The only difference between people with money and those without money is the way they think.

"If you train your mind to think rich thoughts, then you can be rich. But if you train your mind to have poor thoughts, then you'll be poor. Since the white man has always had all the money, he automatically thinks rich thoughts. And since blacks haven't really made a lot of money yet, most of them think poor thoughts. Always think like the person who has all the money.

The second thing you need to do is learn how to listen. Now that doesn't mean listening to these fools who don't have anything around here. You have to listen to the people that have what you want. That means reading their stories and learning how they got rich. If you learn to listen, most people will be glad to share their stories with you. Once you've listened, take the information and make it work. That way, you can learn from other people's mistakes and avoid making the same ones. I promise if you learn to do those two things, there is absolutely nothing you can't accomplish."

I smiled and let those words of wisdom sink deep within my soul. A part of me knew that they were the keys to my success.

As I think about all of the books I've read, the seminars I've attended, and the motivational speeches I've listened to, I believe this lesson from my grandfather is the primary reason I have succeeded in life. I took my grandfather's advice and learned to "think like the white man." Put another way, I learned that thoughts become things and what we think about, we bring about.

When I was in the eleventh grade, I dropped out of high school after attending a seminar where the facilitator convinced me I could get rich selling vacuum cleaners. As I sat in the seminar and listened to the stories of people who had made lots of money selling the vacuum cleaners, I truly believed I could do it also. I'll never forget the excitement as I left the seminar with my first vacuum cleaner. I had begun my journey of entrepreneurship, and it felt absolutely amazing.

Unfortunately, we sometimes make poor choices in life, and this was one of my poor choices. It was a poor decision to drop out of school because I never sold a single vacuum cleaner.

Although it was a poor choice at the time (which I do not regret making), it taught me a valuable lesson. It taught me that

I was not afraid to take risks, and being willing to take risks has been the key to my success.

As I've shared throughout this book, I have overcome some incredible adversities in my life. I'm reminded of a quote, "True success should not be measured by what someone accomplishes in life, but by the obstacles he overcomes while trying to succeed." Based on this quote, I am extremely successful. I have overcome a lot of adversities in my life, and now I have committed to sharing the lessons I've learned along the way with others to help them overcome adversities in their lives. This is my life's purpose, and it is the reason I write books.

The lesson I want to share now is the Four Pillars Of An Extraordinary Life.

Before I share the lesson, I'd like you to answer this question honestly. Do you believe it's possible for a black man to create an extraordinary life?

Be completely honest with yourself. Do you truly believe it's possible?

Believe it or not, your answer to that question determines whether you will be able to build an extraordinary life. Everything begins with your belief that it is possible. If you do not believe it is possible, it will not be possible for you. I'm reminded of a quote by Henry Ford: "Whether you believe you can or whether you believe you can't, you will always be right."

Since you're still reading, I'm going to assume you believe you can, so let's get started.

The key to building an extraordinary life is to recognize these four pillars. The pillars are: inner peace, dynamic health, great relationships, and financial abundance. The word extraordinary can mean different things to different people, but rest assured that if your life is going to be extraordinary, it must have these four pillars.

So, let's break them down.

Inner Peace

Inner peace comes from doing your inner work and understanding who you really are. In order to experience inner peace, you must be willing to get off the societal rollercoaster and learn to trust your inner wisdom. Inner peace is obtained when you learn to unpack your emotional baggage and heal your past traumas. It's about learning to make peace with your past and being in touch with your feelings, thoughts, and beliefs. You will know you have inner peace by how you feel and what you think. You have inner peace if you feel calm, relaxed, optimistic, loving, caring, happy, joyful, forgiving, and content.

You do not have inner peace if you feel stressed, agitated, pessimistic, hateful, selfish, angry, judgmental, and dissatisfied.

If the majority of your thoughts are positive, you will experience inner peace. If most of them are negative, you will not experience inner peace.

One of my favorite quotes says, "If you don't go within, you will always go without." This means you must be willing to look within your heart and mind and check in with your feelings to determine whether or not you are experiencing inner peace.

If you're familiar with the teachings of the master teacher, Jesus Christ, you may remember one of his most powerful lessons in which he said, "Seek first the kingdom of heaven and all things will be given unto you." He then clarified what he meant by saying, "The kingdom of heaven is within you." I believe these quotes point to the truth that the kingdom of heaven is within our hearts and minds, so we must be willing to "go within" to enter the kingdom. This is where inner peace resides.

In order to truly experience inner peace, I also believe you must have a connection to a power greater than yourself. You get to choose your path, but ultimately, you must find the path that is right for you. As I mentioned in a previous chapter, meditation and prayer are practiced in every religion. Therefore, if you truly want to experience inner peace, incorporate these two things into your daily life.

Dynamic Health

It has been said that health is wealth, and this is an undeniable fact. It's also been said that our bodies are our temples, so it is imperative that we take good care of them. Take a moment and think about your health right now. Are you at your ideal weight? Does your body feel good? Do you rely on drugs and medications to get you through the day? Regardless of where you are with your health right now, if you aren't happy with your body, you have the power to change it. Think of your body as the ultimate vehicle. In order to keep a vehicle running smoothly, we must schedule regular maintenance and ensure that if the check engine light is on, we take care of whatever might be wrong with it. Your body is constantly sending you signals if something is wrong with it. If you're overweight, it's your body's way of saying you are taking in more calories than you're burning off, so maybe it's time to burn off some of those calories by exercising or going on a diet. If you have high cholesterol or high blood pressure, it's your body's way of saying something needs to be checked out. If you haven't done so, go to your doctor for a yearly checkup.

Make a commitment to yourself that you will take better care of your body this year and prioritize having dynamic health and a healthy body.

Great Relationships

Relationships are the glue that holds our lives together and it is important that we learn how to nurture and deepen our relationships. Be sure to reread the chapter on relationships and incorporate some of the ideas to help improve your relationships.

Know that relationships do not have to be filled with drama, angst, bitterness, and disappointment. They can be rewarding, fulfilling, satisfying, and fun. It begins with your willingness to create a great relationship with yourself and then find the perfect person to share your life with.

If you're currently not in a relationship, but would like to be, let me suggest that you write out a vision of what you're looking for. It begins by clarifying what qualities and values you are looking for in a partner and then being willing to write those things down in the form of a vision. Once you have the vision, you have to be willing to put forth a little effort to help you attract that person into your life. You can begin by joining a dating site, a singles group, or simply being willing to approach a coworker or associate.

I want to share a vision I wrote back in 1993 when I was looking for my Soulmate. Amazingly, my wife has all of the qualities and values I wrote about and is everything I was looking for in a person to spend the rest of my life with. Although it took me a few years to find her, she was definitely worth the wait, and as mentioned, we have been happily married for 21 years.

Here is my vision.

My Soul-Mate will be intelligent, physically fit, spiritual, and complete within herself.
She will be able to receive all the love I have to give
and also able to give her love freely.
She will be confident and centered and able to allow me the freedom
to be who I am, and I will do the same.
My Soul-Mate will be emotionally honest and trustworthy
and willing to become one with her spiritual equal.
Together we will grow and expand and
support each other in becoming all we were created to be.
She will have a great sense of humor and we will spend hours just laughing and giggling and being silly.
We will take life sincerely but not seriously.
She will love children and accept my children as her own.
We will vow to make our relationship a commitment to God
and therefore create a bond that can never be broken.
Every day will be an acknowledgment of how fortunate we are to have each other
, and we will be committed to growing our relationship through eternity.

We will experience lovemaking at the deepest, most intimate level possible, and each encounter will be an expression of our deep love for one another.
We will travel the world together and experience all the wonders of God's
great creation called earth.
It will be the joining of two complete souls coming together to unite in the love of God!

I wrote this vision on Saturday, 5/15/93, at 6:30 pm. On Tuesday, April 9th, 2002, I married my Soulmate on a beautiful beach on the island of St. Thomas in the Virgin Islands.

Rest assured, if I can find my Soulmate and create the relationship of my dreams, so can you.

Financial Abundance

Financial abundance simply means you have enough money that you don't have to stress out over it. It means being able to do some things you enjoy and purchasing things that you enjoy without worrying about how you will pay for them. Unfortunately, many of us do what Will Smith said, "Too many people spend money they haven't earned to buy things they don't want, to impress people they don't like." You will not get caught in this trap when you are financially abundant. In a lot of cases, the reason people lose control of their finances is because of unfulfilled emotional needs. They believe having "stuff" will make them happy, so they overspend in an attempt to feel happy but are then disappointed when the happiness doesn't last. This creates a vicious cycle that can be difficult to break. Therefore the key is to do your inner work and become happy with yourself, and you are less likely to get caught in the spending trap and trying to fulfill an emotional need.

No matter who you are, where you're from, how much education you have, or what religion you practice, these are the four pillars of an extraordinary life. If you follow the guidelines in this book, I am certain that you, too, can create an extraordinary life.

Creating an extraordinary life can be challenging, so I'd like to close this chapter with five things you can do to ensure you create an extraordinary life.

Key 1: You must be willing to take hundred percent responsibility for your life

That's it! If you are unwilling to do this, you might as well stop reading this book right now. Your success relies on your willingness to take hundred percent responsibility for your life and everything that happens to you. You can't blame your parents, where you were born, or your skin color. You can't blame your lack of education, your ex-spouse, or your age. **You** must decide that you're going to take hundred percent responsibility for your life and then make it happen.

Are you willing to do this?

Of course, this does not mean there won't be people who may hurt you, lie to you, or betray you. It does not mean that there won't be times when you are tired, frustrated, angry, confused, and simply want to give up. It doesn't mean there wont be times when you might try to place blame on the government, society, religion, or the particular culture you were brought up in for being the cause of your failure.

It means you are making a conscious decision right now that you are willing to do whatever it takes. You recognize that if you do not assume hundred percent responsibility for your life, you literally give up your power.

A good way to do this is to remember the Three Cs. Choice, Chance, and Change. It all begins with you, first and foremost, making the choice that you will take hundred percent responsibility for your life to turn out the way you want it to. And then you must make the *choice* to take the *chance* that you can then *change* your life.

Of course, this takes some risk, but with huge risk comes a huge reward, and you must take a chance if you want anything in your life to change.

Make the choice to take a chance if you want your life to change. **Choose right now!**

The Four Pillars Of An Extraordinary Life

So, that's the first key **Take hundred percent responsibility for your life turning out the way you want it to.**

Key 2: **You must be willing to get out of your comfort zone**

Another way to look at getting out of your comfort zone is simply being willing to face your fears. It's been said that fear is the destroyer of dreams, and if you aren't willing to address your fears, you will never be able to accomplish anything of significance.

A wonderful quote states: "You must realize that fear is not real. It is a product of thoughts you create. Do not misunderstand me; danger is real, but fear is a choice.

Fear is a choice. You can choose to let it keep you from accomplishing your goals, or you can feel the fear and do it any way. A powerful acronym for fear is *False Experiences Appearing Real*, which means they are simply thoughts in your mind that appear to be real, yet, they are simply figments of your imagination. They only exist within the framework of your own mind. Getting out of your comfort zone means learning to recognize your fears and not letting them stop you from accomplishing your goals.

Getting out of your comfort zone means being willing to be uncomfortable. As a matter of fact, you must learn to become comfortable with being uncomfortable if you truly want to accomplish extraordinary things in your life.

Key 3: **You must commit to your own growth**

As a human being, you have an infinite learning capacity, and if you're not willing to learn, no one can help you, but if you are determined to learn, no one can stop you either. It is absolutely imperative that you make a commitment to growth. A wonderful saying goes, "If you aren't growing, you're dying." So make a commitment to constant and never-ending improvement, and I can assure you, you'll be able to build an extraordinary life.

Another way to look at growth is by using the computer as a metaphor for your brain. A computer is an amazing technological machine that can be used to do remarkable things. To improve the performance of a computer, you must constantly upgrade software and replace the hardware to keep it running at its maximum potential. Your brain is more powerful than any computer, and you must be willing to constantly upgrade your internal software and take care of your hardware to keep it running at its maximum potential.

Upgrading your inner software means you are willing to look at the subconscious beliefs that may limit your potential. It also means that you are willing to add new programs (beliefs) that can support you in your growth. You can accomplish this by reading books and participating in classes that provide you with the knowledge to accomplish your goals and support you in feeling better about yourself as a human being.

The key is to commit to constant and never-ending improvement in all areas of your life.

Key 4: **You must develop a positive attitude**

So what exactly is attitude? My definition of attitude is, The compilation and expression of your thoughts, feelings, and beliefs. If you have negative beliefs, thoughts, and feelings, you will have a negative attitude. If you have positive thoughts, feelings, and beliefs, you will have a positive attitude. So if you're truly committed to building an extraordinary life, one of the things you have to do is develop a positive attitude because whenever life throws challenges at you, if you have a negative attitude, guess what happens? It's going to make things more difficult for you to deal with. But, if you maintain a positive attitude and if you maintain the idea that you can overcome challenges in your life, then it's going to be much easier for you to turn your adversities into allies. Developing a positive mental attitude is paramount to your success.

Key 5: **You must discover your unique gifts and talents**

Whether you believe this or not, you have very special unique gifts and talents. Chances are you have forgotten what they are, and more than likely, you've given up on sharing them with the world. But rest assured, they are within you. Your goal is to discover these gifts and talents and reignite the inner flame of passion that will allow you to express them. Your gifts are not necessarily something you do – they are primarily about *who you are*. For example, being loving and caring is a gift. Being intelligent and analytical is also a gift. Being ambitious, driven, creative, extraverted, or introverted and compassionate, is a gift.

When you discover your gifts and apply them to your talents, you will find your true purpose. If your gifts are being loving and caring, then your talent could lead you to be a healer or a member of the clergy. If your gifts include intelligence and analytical, your talent could lead you to become a doctor or lawyer. If your gifts include being ambitious and driven, then you may become an entrepreneur or a manager. If you are creative and extraverted, chances are you will become some type of entertainer. If you are introverted and compassionate, then you may choose to become a therapist or counselor.

Get the picture?

Your gifts are lying dormant within you. It is your responsibility to wake them up. No one can discover or express them for you, and you must commit to discovering them for yourself. When you do, I can assure you that you will not only be able to fully express yourself authentically, but also find joy and passion in everything you do.

Find your gifts and express your talents, and you can live a rewarding and fulfilling life.

The Four Pillars Of An Extraordinary Life

So to recap, the five keys are:

1: Take hundred percent responsibility for your life.
2: Get out of your comfort zone.
3: You must commit to your own growth.
4: You must develop a positive attitude.
5: You must discover your unique gifts and talents.

Just remember, creating an extraordinary life begins with your willingness to believe it is possible for you and then being willing to do whatever it takes to create the life of your dreams. Once you make that decision, you're already halfway there.

You got this!

"We are shaped by our thoughts; we become what we think. When the mind is pure, joy follows like a shadow that never leaves."
– Buddha

Chapter 11

Don't Forget To Have Some Fun

I once gave a presentation titled Living With Joy. In the speech, I talked about the importance of having and expressing joy and shared some of the reasons many men struggle with being able to feel joy and express it.

After the presentation, a man walked up to me and said he didn't trust me and didn't believe what I said about it being possible for any man to find joy. I asked him why he didn't trust me, and he said his father taught him never to trust a man who smiles too much. He said men who smiled were always hiding something, and therefore, he had made up his mind that any man who smiled all the time was untrustworthy. He shared with me how difficult his life had been and commented that he had absolutely nothing to be happy about.

Don't Forget To Have Some Fun

There was a lot of sadness and anger on his face, and I felt a deep compassion for him. I asked him if he wanted to sit down and talk, and he agreed. I went into detail again about all the adversities I'd been through in my own life and shared my emotional healing journey with him and how I had found my joy. As I shared my story, I noticed he began to soften up just a little, and I knew he was beginning to accept some of the things I was saying. By the time we finished our conversation, he was a completely different person. It was probably the first time anyone had really listened to him without judgment and simply created a safe enough space for him to get some things off of his chest. I was able to get him to see that he, too, could find his joy, but he would have to be willing to change his belief about men who smiled. It was that single belief that had kept him from finding his joy. By speaking with me and finding out that I was sincere and trustworthy, he could reframe that belief which opened the door to him finding his joy. After our conversation, he even smiled and commented that it had been a long time since he had something to smile about.

As men of color, it may seem as if we don't have anything to smile about. Once again, if we pay attention to the CWBS media, it will convince us that the challenges we face are insurmountable, and therefore, there is no reason for us to smile or be happy. You must understand and accept that it is your responsibility to find your joy. You will never find it through mainstream media and you will never find it through being around negative people. You will only find it when you become willing to do your inner work of uncovering any hidden emotional traumas you may have experienced and become willing to heal those traumas.

It goes back to what I said about energy. If you aren't feeling your joy, it's because it is covered up with negative emotions. Maybe you're carrying around a lot of anger and rage. Or maybe your heart is filled with sadness. Whatever it is, you will not access your joy until you become willing to heal that negative energy.

So the first step in finding your joy is to do your inner work and remove any negative emotions that may be blocking your joy. (Be sure to reread chapter 3)

That said, I'd like to ask you when was the last time you had fun. There are several different ways to have fun, but I'd like you to consider the last time you did anything you thought was fun.

As you think about that experience, ask yourself how you honestly felt during the time you were doing it. Were you smiling and laughing? Did it feel good?

If you're trapped on the rollercoaster, there is a possibility you may think you're having fun when in reality, you aren't. Here is an example. Let's imagine you go to a club and hanging out with friends. It appears that you're having fun because you're hanging out with your buddies, and you have your favorite drink. Now, let's imagine you have too much to drink and become intoxicated. So you are staggering around before you realize you should probably go home. Of course, your friends are telling you to stay and have another drink, but you've had enough, and you know you really should be on your way home.

Now let's imagine you get home safely (thank God) and you first run to the toilet to puke. After puking your guts out, you hobble to your bedroom and crash out on your bed. The following day you wake up with a massive headache and hangover, and it takes the whole day to recover fully.

The next time you talk to your friends, they ask you how you're doing, and you respond by saying how much fun you had at the club and how you can't wait to do it again.

Now ask yourself honestly, did you really have fun?

There is definitely nothing wrong with drinking alcohol and hanging out with friends. But when you're trapped on the rollercoaster, you will rationalize getting drunk as having fun. Before I jumped off the rollercoaster, the hypothetical story I just shared happened to me. I went to a club with some friends, got wasted, barely made it home without having an accident, got home and hugged the toilet for twenty minutes, and didn't even make it to my bed before I passed out on the floor. The next day it felt like my head exploded. As I sat there with my throbbing headache, I had an epiphany. At that moment, I realized being drunk was not fun, and from that moment on, I made a conscious choice not to drink alcohol. It's been over thirty years since I have had an alcoholic drink, and I must admit I've never missed drinking alcohol.

The point of the story is, being drunk isn't fun. We can rationalize and justify it as having fun and relaxing, but if we are one hundred percent honest with ourselves, there is nothing fun about being wasted.

Here's a question for you. What do you do for fun? What are your hobbies? What is it that you love to do?

Unfortunately, most of us as men focus all our energy and effort on our jobs, relationships, and families, but we don't know how to take time for ourselves and do things for our own enjoyment. The truth is, most men simply do not know how to have fun. What about you? Do you know how to have fun?

Another way to look at having fun is to find your creative outlet. Believe it or not, you are creative. Different people will express their creativity differently, but every human being is creative. The challenge for you is to find your creative outlet and then go out and create something. Creativity can show up through cooking, drawing, building, singing, writing, or even serving others. You are responsible for finding and expressing your creativity. A great way to find your creativity is by knowing what you love to do. Your creativity will naturally follow when you find what you love to do. So how do you find out what you love to do? Here are three ways to know if you're doing what you love.

1-When you are doing what you love, you will do it without considering compensation. In other words, you do it for the pure joy of it, and you aren't concerned with whether or not you will benefit from it in any way. Your joy is its own reward, and you're doing it simply because you love to. This does not necessarily mean you can't get paid for doing what you love; it means you do it without thinking about making money.

2-When you are doing what you love, time literally disappears, and you lose track of time. You become so engaged in what you're doing that time just flies by.

3-When you do what you love, you want to share it with others. Expressing your creativity with others brings you joy, and knowing you are bringing joy to others is loads of fun.

So, what do you love to do? Are you having fun? Are you expressing your creativity? If not, now is a great time to begin. Commit to having fun and expressing your creativity, and I can assure you that you will experience pure unadulterated joy.

That said, I want to share some of the things I do for fun. As you're reading my list, take notes and see if there are some things on the list you might like to do yourself. If there are, here is a great opportunity to have some fun, so follow my lead and do them for yourself.

Writing is my passion! I love books and have always enjoyed reading. Although I never dreamed of becoming an author when I was younger, I learned how to nurture my love of writing by becoming an author. When I'm writing, time disappears. I can sit at my computer for hours, and it honestly feels like minutes.

In conjunction with writing, I also love teaching. Teaching allows me to share my knowledge with others. There are few things more rewarding than having someone tell me how my books have positively impacted their lives which is the primary reason I write books in the first place. They give me an opportunity to help other people.

Public speaking is also one of my passions. I love being on stage, sharing insights and wisdom with others to support them in building extraordinary lives.

I am also a huge movie buff. I absolutely love going to the movies. My wife and I go about two times a month because we both have a passion for movies. This leads me to another thing I do for fun: hang out with my wife. We always reserve

Don't Forget To Have Some Fun

Fridays as our date day. Each Friday, we make it a point to spend quality time together.

Another thing we enjoy doing together is traveling. We have been blessed to have traveled abroad and visited several different countries. We've taken a couple of cruises and are currently planning another international trip now that COVID-19 is no longer a pandemic. We both love to travel!

Another passion of mine is music. As a former DJ, I have always loved music, and I love listening to old school '70s and '80s music, like, Cameo, Confunkshun, Rick James, Parliament, Teddy Pendergrass, and Luther Vandross.

These are a few of the things I do for fun, and now I'd like to challenge you to come up with your own list.

Take a moment and write down five things you do for fun.

1. _____
2. _____
3. _____
4. _____
5. _____

Were you able to come up with five things? If the answer is no, here is the perfect opportunity to figure out what you like to do and then take Nike's advice and just do it!

Always remember, you are hundred percent responsible for having fun. It's up to you to decide what fun looks like but make sure you're incorporating some fun into your life, and I can assure you everyone around you will be happier when you do.

Don't forget to have some fun!

"Everybody can be great... because anybody can serve. You don't have to have a college degree to serve. You don't have to make your subject and verb agree to serve. You only need a heart full of grace. A soul generated by love."
– Martin Luther King Jr.

Chapter 12

Be Willing To Serve

It's been said that "To whom much is given, much is expected." If you are blessed with financial abundance, then a way to acknowledge that abundance is to give some away. There is a law called the law of reciprocity, which basically means what you put out will come back to you or be reciprocated. When you give love, you receive love. When you share kindness, you receive kindness. When you give money, you receive money. This is a universal law that works every time, but you have to believe and trust in it to have it work for you.

The best way to do this is to give with an open heart without any expectation of return. If you give some money, don't think in the back of your mind, I'm going to get some money back. Simply count your blessings that you have it to give away and be grateful that you were able to help someone less fortunate than you. When you surrender to this law, the Universe will bless you in countless ways, and your blessings will overflow.

Be Willing To Serve

Even if you only have a dollar to give, you will be blessed immeasurably if you do it with an open heart and an open mind.

Always remember to give something back! Giving back is another way of being in service.

It is my contention that every human being has a divine purpose. I also believe that we show up with everything we need to fulfill that purpose; unfortunately, most people do not find nor fulfill their purpose because we live in a world that constantly tells us to "look outside" of ourselves for happiness and happiness fulfillment.

In other words, we pursue external things like money, cars, titles, sex, work, and relationships because we believe these things will make us happy and provide security. Our focus is always "out there" instead of "in here."

Probably the most difficult thing we will ever do is to change our focus and become self-introspective, which means taking a look within our own hearts and minds to discover who we really are and why we are here. It isn't until we commit to doing this that we can find true fulfillment, passion, and purpose.

For those who follow the Christian religion, you may recall Jesus saying, "Seek ye first the kingdom of Heaven, and all things will be given unto you." He then clarified what he meant by saying, "The kingdom of Heaven does not come from your careful observation. You cannot say here it is or there it is because the kingdom of Heaven is within you!"

The kingdom of Heaven is within you, and you are responsible for entering that kingdom and finding your passion and purpose.

So how does a person find their purpose?

Earlier in this book, I invited you to make peace with yourself, so you can know yourself. This is the key to finding your purpose. Before you do anything else, you must take this first step. Knowing thyself means fully understanding who you are as a human being. It means understanding your strengths and weaknesses. It means knowing your values; it means knowing what you truly believe about yourself, life, and the world around you. It is about knowing how you feel and being able to express your feelings. It is about facing your fears and being willing to do whatever it takes to move through them.

It is an inner journey that few people will take, but if you're reading this right now, you are one of those few.

Once you Know Thyself, there are two things you have to do to find your purpose.

1. You must discover your passion and the things you love to do.

Be Willing To Serve

2. You must apply your passions to help make the world a better place.

In the previous chapter, I shared three ways to know that you are doing what you love. Another way of describing this is by finding your passions. Finding what you love to do and finding your passions are the same thing, so let me share those three ways to know when you're doing what you love once again. The first way to know if you're doing what you love is that time literally disappears when you're doing it. The second way to know is that you will do it without the thought of compensation. In other words, you simply do it because you love doing it, and it doesn't matter if you get paid for doing it. Doing it brings you joy and lights you up.

The third way of knowing is that you want to share what you do with others. Taking what you love and sharing it with others warms your heart and gives you a sense of meaning and purpose. It doesn't matter what it is you're doing; what matters is that you love doing it.

Your challenge is to find out what you love to do.

Once you've found out, the next step is to take what you love to do and figure out how to help or serve others. For example, I love writing. By sharing my knowledge with others through my books, I am serving others by inspiring them to reach their full potential. So I take my passion, which is writing, then I share my writing with others to help improve their lives, and in doing so, I am making the world a better place.

So, Passion + Service = Purpose

It's simple but not easy. But I can assure you that it is doable for you.

You must understand there is no purpose that is bigger or better than another person's purpose. There is only "your" purpose. Do not try and compare yourself to others. Find out what you love to do, serve others, and you will fulfill your purpose.

Another way to find your purpose is to simply begin doing something that helps other people. For example, you could go to a homeless shelter and help serve food. While you're there, you may find out that you love serving food, and that could become your purpose.

Or maybe you could mentor a child and help them stay on the right track, and then you find out that you love teaching, and that could be your purpose.

What if you went to an old folks' home and spent some time with someone who has no family and would simply love some company? Could your purpose be counseling and consoling others?

Or maybe there is a family member or a co-worker who has been struggling financially, and you know that you could support them in some way with some financial support. Your purpose could be giving.

Do you know how to fix cars or repair homes, and can you share that knowledge with someone? Your purpose could be sharing your expertise.

Could you take three hours a week, go to an elementary school, and read to young children? Your purpose could be found in that elementary school.

There are literally thousands of things you can do right now to serve your community. It's time for you to find your passion and your purpose so that you can be in service.

What the world needs right now are people who are willing to be of service to humanity. The world is crying out for positive voices who are committed to making the world a better place.

As men who happen to be black, we have an excellent opportunity to allow our voices to be heard and encourage others to live extraordinary lives. No longer can we play victims and wait for others to help us resolve our problems. It's up to us now, and I hope that this book has inspired you to take positive action.

I know without question that every man has the capacity to live an extraordinary life, and Black men are no different from any other men. What has been missing are the resources to support them in reaching their full potential, and I have made it my life's work to provide some of those resources.

I want to thank you for taking the time to read this book. Now the real work begins. You must apply what you have learned to your own life and commit to making it extraordinary. Once you do, reach one and teach one and pass it on.

Always remember, Black men are thriving and experiencing unprecedented levels of success today, so now it's your turn to join them by creating the life of your dreams.

Good luck!

Coach Michael Taylor

Bio's

Coach Michael Taylor

Michael *is an entrepreneur, author (12 books), motivational speaker, certified life coach, podcaster, and radio and TV show host who has dedicated his life to empowering men and women to reach their full potential by transforming their lives from the inside out. He knows first hand how to overcome adversity and build a rewarding and fulfilling life and he is sharing his knowledge and wisdom with others to support them in creating the* life of their dreams. www.coachmichaeltaylor.com

He was featured in the bestselling book Motivational Speakers America with speaking legends Les Brown and Brian Tracey, and he is also an Amazon.com bestselling author. He has won numerous awards for his dynamic speaking style and he has been featured on multiple radio and TV interviews across the country. (see website)

He is President & CEO of Creation Publishing Group which is a company that specializes in creating programs and products that empower men and women to create extraordinary lives and he currently hosts three television channels on the Roku Television Network.

Most importantly he has been blissfully married for 20 years to the woman of his dreams and he is a proud father to three grown children whom he is extremely proud of.

When he isn't writing or speaking you'll find him checking out the latest movies or listening to old school 70's and 80's soul music and contemporary jazz.

He considers himself to be an irrepressible optimist with a passion for the impossible and he believes there has never been a better time to be alive on this planet than right now.

Paul Randolph Newell

Paul *is a Soul that is intent on co-creating a heart-full culture of Men by guiding himself and other Men to vibrate authentically in body, mind, and spirit. His intention is at the core of his work in health and well-being, human resources, and group facilitation.*

He is a Men's Health and Well-Being Guide working with **The Mankind Project** *and* **All Kings**. *He facilitates personal development and empowerment courses for men to support them in enhancing emotional intelligence, communication, and connection. He is also the Creator and Host of the* **MenTalk About** *podcast, designed to guide men in their education, development and inner work to live a life of purpose and fulfillment.*

Bio's

Paul has written and published the book, **The Heal.Thy.Man Method** *to support the education, healing and self-awareness enhancement of Men to transcend systemic conditioning and perceptions to live a life of clarity, purpose, abundance and health.*

He also has 20 years of corporate experience in human resources, public speaking, learning and development, and coaching. While he worked in a corporate setting, he fueled his passion for health and wellness by teaching yoga and fitness classes, and delivering health and wellness workshops in various communities. He currently manages and co-hosts a weekly call for men of color to discuss topics that are relevant and resonant for our communities

He is also an experienced Yoga Teacher with 300hr and 500hr Certifications and over ten year's experience teaching classes and co-facilitating yoga teacher trainings. He leverages his knowledge and experience to guide others to find their strength and resiliency in their body, mind, and spirit.

Connect with Paul via email at paul@healthymanmethod.com or via his IG account @newellnessmensguide

Jermaine Johnson

Jermaine *was born and raised in St. Albans Queens, New York. He moved to Atlanta in 1996 and has owned and operated a successful business there since 2006. He has consulted with many startup companies and mentored Young Black entrepreneurs.*

Jermaine joined The Mankind Project USA (MKP) in 2015 and since then has been instrumental in coordinating and empowering Men of Color within the organization. He organized, led, and still leads the 1st official Society for People of Color within MKP in 2020. Jermaine created the 1st Intensive weekend for Men of Color in MKP with an All Black Leader Team and all Men of Color on Staff. This intensive, initiatory weekend is known as The New Warrior Training Adventure (NWTA) and is based on African Tribal Traditions, Ceremonies, and Rituals.

Bio's

Jermaine is formally trained by "Visions Inc". The leader in exploring the impacts of Racism on society in the United States. This training, and Jermaine's Facilitation training, make him uniquely qualified to lead large rooms of diversity and handle any triggers or wounding that can potentially occur. He has extensive experience in leading circles, workshops, and training as well as creating the content, curriculum, and schedules for any venue large or small.

Jermaine is the CoFounder of The Brothahood of Kings Collective (BKC). This initiative began in 2021 with an emphasis on Outreach, Facilitation Training, Leadership Training, and Intercultural Competency. Jermaine's experience and personal skills have contributed to the growth and success of the BKC.

Jermaine currently holds the following roles in The Mankind Project.

- *Curriculum Developer for People of Color*
- *Circle Support for the Chairman*
- *Intercultural Advocate*
- *Executive Director*
- *Facilitator*
- *Trainer*
- *Leader*

kbh.mkp@gmail.com
jermainejohnson@mkp.org
Twitter@brothahoodofkings

The Brothahood of Kings

Greg "Reimoku" Smith

Gregory Reimoku Smith (he/him) is a student and disciple in the Zen Buddhist lineage of Taisen Deshimaru and Kodo Sawaki. With over thirteen years of formal experience, he has chosen zazen as his practice and the world as his dojo. As a highly sensitive, queer, Black man, he engages deeply with life and the nuanced perspectives these identities afford him. Reimoku graduated with honors from Tulane University in 2016 with a B.A. in the Humanities and currently resides in New Orleans, LA. Having a gift for languages and wordsmithing, he makes a living as a Spanish translator and interpreter. As a Contemplative Coach for the Mature Masculine and co-founder of BKC, his mission is to support men, especially Black highly sensitives, in leading an authentically liberated life with wisdom, compassion, and a courageous tenderness.

Email: zenfriendurbanmonk@gmail.com
Instagram: zenfriend.urbanmonk

Resources

www.brothahoodofkings.com

Coach Michael Taylor sites:
www.coachmichaeltaylor.com
www.shatterthestereotypes.com
www.onlynesscure.com
www.jesuswasacoach.com
www.adversityisyourgreatestally.com
www.anewconversationwithmen.com
www.creationpublishing.com (Company Website)
www.stssummit.com

Email: mtaylor@coachmichaeltaylor.com

Paul Newell sites;
https://www.linkedin.com/in/paulrnewell/
https://www.healthymanmethod.com/
https://anchor.fm/mentalkabout
https://www.youtube.com/user/BalancedWellnessLLC/

Books by Coach Michael Taylor

www.ingramcontent.com/pod-product-compliance
Lightning Source LLC
Chambersburg PA
CBHW070656120526
44590CB00013BA/988